THE GENIUS

OF

THE COMMON LAW

BY

THE RIGHT HONORABLE

SIR FREDERICK POLLOCK, BART, D C L., LL.D.

OF LINCOLN'S INN, BARRISTER AT LAW; HONORARY FELLOW
OF CORPUS CHRISTI COLLEGE, OXFORD

THE LAWBOOK EXCHANGE, LTD.
Clark, New Jersey

ISBN 978-1-58477-043-5

Lawbook Exchange edition 2000, 2019

The quality of this reprint is equivalent to the quality of the original work.

THE LAWBOOK EXCHANGE, LTD.
33 Terminal Avenue
Clark, New Jersey 07066-1321

*Please see our website for a selection of our other publications
and fine facsimile reprints of classic works of legal history:*
www.lawbookexchange.com

Library of Congress Cataloging-in-Publication Data

Pollock, Frederick, Sir, 1845-1937.
　　The genius of the common law / by Sir Frederick Pollock.
　　　　p.　cm.
　　Originally published: New York : Columbia University Press, 1912.
　　(Columbia University lectures. The Carpentier lectures ; 1911).
　　Includes bibliographical references and index.
　　ISBN 1-58477-043-0 (acid-free paper)
　　　1. Common law. I. Title. II. Columbia University lectures. Carpentier
　　lectures; 11.

K588.P65　2000
340.5'7--dc21　　　　　　　　　　　　　　　　　99-047160

Printed in the United States of America on acid-free paper

COLUMBIA UNIVERSITY LECTURES

THE GENIUS

OF

THE COMMON LAW

BY

THE RIGHT HONORABLE

SIR FREDERICK POLLOCK, BART, D C L., LL.D.

OF LINCOLN'S INN, BARRISTER AT LAW; HONORARY FELLOW
OF CORPUS CHRISTI COLLEGE, OXFORD

New York
THE COLUMBIA UNIVERSITY PRESS
1912

PREFACE

THE purpose of the Carpentier Lectures is not to furnish text-books for ordinary professional use, and I have therefore not thought it proper to cite authorities except for a few historical illustrations too lately published to be familiar, or otherwise off the usual lines. Once or twice I have named a leading case for the convenience of learned readers. I do not think I have positively stated anything as law which will not be well known to any such reader, and easily verified if desired; and the same remark applies to the historical data.

F. P.

CONTENTS

I. OUR LADY AND HER KNIGHTS

MORE than seven years have passed since I was invited to speak here in the name of our Common Law. The renewal of such an invitation is if possible more honourable than its first proffer, and it would seem a simple matter to accept it with alacrity. But it comes from the young, nay from the immortals — for are not incorporate universities immortal? — to a man who must soon be irrevocably called old if he is not already so; a man at whose age the lapse of days gives a little more warning of some kind at every solstice, and whom it tells among other things that his outlook on life and doctrine is pretty well fixed for better or worse. Such a man cannot expect to acquire fresh points of view or to frame novel conceptions of any value. He may hope, at best, to keep an open mind for the merits of younger men's discoveries; to find in the store of his experience, now and then, something that may help them on the way; to sort out results of thought and observation not yet set in order, and make them of some little use, if it may be, to his fellow-students; perhaps even to bring home to some others the grounds of his faith in the science of law, the faith that it has to do not with a mere intellectual craft but with a vital aspect of human and national history.

When I say human, I mean to lay on that word rather more than its bare literal import. I mean to rule out, so far as one man can do it, the old pretence that a lawyer is bound to regard the system he was trained in, whether it be the Common Law or any other, as a monster of inhuman

perfection. Indeed the whole theme of these lectures will
include as one chief purpose the development of this protest.
Laymen may still be found to say in bewilderment or dis-
appointment, as Mr. Justice Hillary said, we may presume in
jest, towards the middle of the fourteenth century, that law
is what the justices will; and we are still ready to reply with
his brother judge Stonore: 'No: law is reason.'[1] Reason
let it be, the best we can discover in our day. But the dogmatic assertion that law is the perfection of reason belongs
to a later age, an age of antiquarian reverence often falling
into superstition and of technical learning often corrupted
by pedantry. We are here to do homage to our lady the
Common Law; we are her men of life and limb and earthly
worship. But we do not worship her as a goddess exempt
from human judgment or above human sympathy. She
is no placid Madonna sitting in a rose garden; rather she
is like the Fortitude of the Florentine master, armed and
expectant; her battle-mace lightly poised in fingers ready to
close, at one swift motion, to the fighting grasp. Neither
is she a cold minister of the Fates. Her soul is founded in
an order older than the gods themselves, but the joy of strife
is not strange to her, nor yet the humours of the crowd. She
belongs to the kindred of Homer's gods, more powerful than
men but not passionless or infallible. She can be jealous
with Hera, merciless with Artemis, and astute with Athena.
She can jest with her servants on occasion. I would not
warrant that she hid her face, any more than Queen Elizabeth
would have done, even at those merry sayings of Chief Justice Bereford which Maitland might not translate. She

---

[1] R. Thorpe (arg.) . autrement nous ne savoms ceo qe la ley est. — HILL.
Volunte des Justices. — STON-NANYL , ley est resoun. Y. B., 18–19 Ed. III
(A.D. 1345), ed. Pike (Rolls series, 1905), p. 378.

has never renounced pomps and vanities. On the contrary, she delights in picturesque variety of symbols and ceremonial up to the point where it becomes inconvenient, and sometimes a little way beyond. Her expounders may dwell on forms with a certain loving solemnity, as Littleton where he says: 'Homage is the most honourable service, and most humble service of reverence, that a frank tenant may do to his lord.' But they need not always be solemn. Our lady was not enthroned in the Middle Ages for nothing. Like a true medieval clerk, she can indite an edifying tale or a devout comment and make a grotesque figure in the margin. Yet I have known good English lawyers who can see nothing but barbarism in the Middle Ages. I suspect those learned friends of being, I will not say possessed, but in some measure obsessed, by the enemy; not a medieval fiend with horns and claws, but a more dangerous one, the polished and scholarly Mephistopheles of the Romanizing Renaissance. Once he broke his teeth, as Maitland has shown us, on the tough law that the Inns of Court had made. But he is not dead, and our lady the Common Law has had other brushes with him, and may have shrewd ones yet. Now this brings me to the pith and sum of my enterprise, which is to consider her adventures in these and other perils, early and late: adventures of heroic mould and beyond any one man's competence, but not so facile as to be wanting in dramatic interest, or to fail of mixing warning with ensample. We shall find her achievements and her mishaps not less varied than those of pilgrims or knights errant in general, some of them, I think, as surprising as anything in romance. She has faced many foes and divers manner of weapons; she knows as much as Bunyan's Christian of Apollyon's fiery darts and Giant Despair's grievous crab-tree cudgel.

Some one, however, may say that if we consider our lady the Common Law too curiously, we may move another kind of curiosity to profane questioning whether she is a person at all; and if we fail to prove her reality (which probably cannot be done to the satisfaction of a common jury of lay people), peradventure we may be in mercy for bringing her into contempt as some sort of *persona ficta*, or yet worse, that useless figment of shreds and patches, a corporation sole. It may be safer to drop romance for a time and betake ourselves to the usual abstractions of serious discourse, while not admitting that they bring us much nearer to reality. Wherever we find a named and organic body of any kind, a nation, a church, a profession, a regiment, a college or academic institution, even a club, which has lasted long enough to have a history continued for more than a generation or two, we shall hardly fail to find also something analogous to that which in a single human being is called character; abilities, dispositions, usage that may be counted on. Such bodies acquire a reputation in respect not only of capacity, solvency, or businesslike habits, but of taste and temper. They may be enlightened or stupid, pleasant or unpleasant to deal with. In fact collective tradition and custom may give rise in a corporate unit (not confining the attribute to its strictly legal sense) to a stronger and more consistent character than is shown by most individuals. There is no alternative but to say that a commonwealth and all its subordinate and co-ordinate parts are nothing but a concourse of human atoms, and social history nothing more than a succession of accidents; in other words to deny that there is any political or legal science at all beyond a bare dogmatic analysis of the facts as taken at a given date and assumed (of course falsely) to be stationary. Thus we should

be like amateur collectors of minerals, ignoring the structure
of the earth and making an arbitrary arrangement of speci-
mens on the shelves of a cabinet. I confess to a deep want
of interest in shelves for their own sake. But really discussion seems prétty superfluous here and now; for if the
better opinion were that history is a mere *hortus siccus* of
documents and anecdotes, there would be no reason why
I should be here at all, or, being here, why there should be
any one to listen to me. So let us take it as decided, for
the purpose of this course at any rate, that we accept the
hypothesis of a real continuity. That being our position,
we must further take it as true that not only men but institutions and doctrines have a life history. Given, then, an
actual moral development (without assuming that it is uniform in direction, or always for the better), we cannot regard
it as development of nothing; the facts must express a spiritual unity for us whether we can define it or not. In our
Faculty we are taught to beware of definition, and therefore
as prudent lawyers we may content ourselves with a symbol.
None better occurs to me than the old Roman one of the
Genius, a symbolic personage who is not to be conceived
exactly as a heathen guardian angel, for he is not only a
minister of grace or persuader to virtue, nor invariably favourable. He combines all elements of fortune, and is rather
an unseen comrade on a higher plane, *natale comes qui tem-
perat astrum*, than a master or mentor. We may call him a
clarified image of the earthly self, a self represented as bringing forth the fruit of its best possible efficiency, but always
of its own, not of any better or other qualities than those it
actually has. Our Genius may stand also for a protest
against another erroneous view, that which, out of zeal to
avoid the inconsequence of the mere story-teller, would set

up a rigid external fatalism.   If this were right, history would
be not only inevitable (which everything is when it has
happened) but a pure logical deduction from predetermined
ideas, if only we had the key to that kind of logic.   But it
is not so, for the short reason that, even if a superhuman
intelligence could formulate a calculus of human action, it
could not do so without counting the men.   Experience tells
us that character does count, whatever else does, and what
is more, that it is often decisive at the most critical points.
Habit will serve a traveler on the plain road; character is
tested when it comes to a parting of the ways.   This has
nothing to do with any metaphysical controversy.   For
surely no pleader for determinism will assert that the determining causes of human action are confined to external
motives, nor will any sane advocate of free will deny that,
when action has to be taken upon one's judgment of what
a man is likely to do, some knowledge of his former conduct
and his character will be found useful.   All the great moralists are at one in ascribing perfect freedom only to the man
(if such a man there can be) who may do his pleasure because
his will, being wholly purified, can be pleased only in what
is right.   Such an one is crowned and consecrated his own lord
in things both temporal and spiritual, as it was said to Dante
when he had passed through Purgatory.   He is beyond any
particular rules because the very nature of his will is to fulfil
all righteousness.   His action could be foretold with certainty by any one who knew the facts and had the same
sense of right, and yet no man would contend that he is not
free.   So much passing remark seems to be called for to
avoid any charge of meddling with high matters of philos-
ophy beyond the scope of our undertaking.   For the rest,
we can expect no such good fortune as to meet with ideal

types of perfection in our journeyings on the ground of actual history.

In the sense and for the causes I have now shortly set forth, I propose as the general subject of these lectures the Genius of the Common Law. For reasons which seem imperative, I do not propose to handle the matter as a chronicler. A concise history of the Common Law might be a very good thing; I have thought once and again of its possibilities; but if ever the time comes when it can be brought within the compass of eight, ten or twelve lectures, it will be after much more searching and sifting have been done. At present my learned friend Dr. Holdsworth of Oxford has brought us down to the sixteenth century in three substantial but not unhandy volumes. We do not know that he, or any man, could have made the story shorter with safety; we do know that it grew in the author's hands to be a good deal longer than at first he meant it to be; we know too that our time now disposable is short. I shall assume therefore that I speak to hearers not ignorant in a general way of the lines on which our common stock of judicial and legal tradition has been formed. Supposing the road and the country to be known to that extent, we will examine a certain number of the critical adventures our fathers met with in their pilgrimage; we will observe their various fortunes on different occasions, and see what may be learnt for our profit from their success or failure.

We must begin, however, at the beginning. It is easy to say that the law of our modern courts, for most practical intents, is to be found in the decisions and statutes of the last half century or thereabouts, and the rest is antiquarianism; and if some people say this in England, I suppose it is at least as often said in America, perhaps with more colour of reason;

though even here I would remind learned friends that there have been boundary disputes between States involving interpretation of the original colonial charters and intricate questions of old real property law. But now we are considering the permanent mind and temper of the Common Law, not the particular rules which judges administer to-day. The branches grow indeed, but they have always grown from the same roots; and those roots must be sought for as far back as the customs of the Germanic tribes who confronted the Roman legions when Britain was still a Roman province and Celtic.   The description of Tacitus is familiar [1] : one passage in his 'Germania' has been a crux of scholars for generations, and is not yet fully or finally cleared up; but we cannot pass on without a glance at the broad features of the Teutonic institutions as he shows them. We need not dwell on the question how far he purposely made out an exaggerated contrast with the manners of imperial Roman society. No one has charged him with downright invention, and we are concerned here with the type — 'the ideal of the Teutonic system' in Stubbs's words — and not with individual cases. Doubtless it was better realized in some tribes and clans than in others; the extent of the variations does not matter for the present purpose. Taking the Germans as described by Tacitus, we find among them a life of great publicity, with personal command only in war time, and ultimate decision, as distinct from executive authority and preliminary counsel, in the hands of the free men assembled in arms. The family is monogamous. Morals are simple and, by comparison with Greek or Roman habits,

---

[1] It may be a great question for ethnologists, but seems irrelevant for us here, whether the people comprised in it were all of like race, and to what extent of unmixed race. Tradition is more important for the matter in hand than actual descent.

extremely strict;[1] for cowardice and effeminate vice there
is no mercy. Gambling, on the other hand, is unrestrained,
and adventurousness encouraged. Women not only exhort
men to valour but are consulted in affairs of weight, though
not in public.[2] The external conditions are as different as
can be from those of urban and commercial civilized life as
they have existed in modern times and even in the Middle
Ages. With so great a change of environment, we might
expect the results to have been transformed almost beyond
recognition. And yet, when we look at the modern social
ethics of Europe and North America, can we fail to recognize
a considerable persistence of the type? That persistence was
in some respects reinforced by the teaching of the Christian
church after the conversion of the Roman empire; in others,
on the contrary, Germanic custom has been pretty stubborn
in the face of ecclesiastical discouragement. It would seem
that the not uncommon practice of treating all the virtues
we profess to cultivate as distinctively Christian is not altogether just. Who taught us respect for women? Our
heathen ancestors. Who laid down for us the faith that the
life of a free nation is public, and its actions bear lasting
fruit because they are grounded in the will of the people?
Our heathen ancestors. Who bade us not only hate but des-
pise the baser forms of vice, and hold up an ideal of clean
and valiant living which European Christianity could as-

[1] 'We may easily discover that Tacitus indulges an honest pleasure in the
contrast of barbarian virtue with the dissolute conduct of the Roman ladies;
yet there are some striking circumstances that give an air of truth, or at
least of probability, to the conjugal faith and chastity of the Germans.'
Gibbon, c. ix.

[2] The passage referred to (c. 8) is so brief as to leave in some obscurity
both what the facts were and how Tacitus understood them. Some anthropologists think the words 'sanctum aliquid et providum' point to a survival
of prehistoric magical beliefs or of matriarchal observance. That there is
a religious element of some kind is clear enough.

similate, so becoming a creed not only of God-fearing but of self-respecting men? Our heathen ancestors. Among those ancestors we may count, besides the Germans, the Scandinavians, whose invasions contributed in a notable proportion to the English stock of descent. Their customs, about the time of the Norman Conquest, were still much like those described in the 'Germania.' Regularity and even formality had been introduced in public business, but there was no defined executive power.

Now there are two cautions to be observed here. First, it would be foolish to claim for the Teutonic nations or kindred an exclusive title to any one of the qualities noted by Tacitus. Taken singly, we may find parallels to most of them in various regions of the world at various times. The Greeks described by Homer, for example, are much nearer to the Germanic ideal than Plato's contemporaries; and it is more than probable that in the Germans Tacitus found a living image of regretted virtues which were believed to have flourished under the Roman republic. Other analogies have no doubt existed in other branches of the Indo-European family, and among people who are not Indo-European at all. It is enough to mention the Celts of the dimly discerned heroic age — the days to which the legendary disputes of Ossian and Patrick were assigned — and the Arabs of the time before Islam. But it remains a notable and, I think, a singular fact that the Germanic type was preserved as a whole, and so little affected by foreign influence, at the very time when the civilization of the Mediterranean lands had become cosmopolitan, and both Hellenic and Roman manners were infected with Asiatic corruption as well as Asiatic enthusiasm. Whatever may be the right explanation of this, the constant affection of the Common Law for both freedom and publicity does appear to owe something to it. The second caution is that, in claiming justice for our pagan ancestors, I have no desire to be less than just to the Church. There is no ground for any polemical inference. All the Germanic virtues, in so far as they agree with the precepts and commendations of the Church, belong to the law of nature in the regular scholastic usage of the term: that is to say, they are the following of general rules binding on all men as moral and rational beings, and discoverable by human reason without any special aid of revelation. According to the accepted teaching of the Schoolmen, if I am rightly informed, there is no sufficient cause, indeed no excuse, for man even in his fallen state not to know the law of nature; his defect is not in understanding but in will, and his works are unacceptable for want of obedience rather than of knowledge. What we have said, therefore, of the unconverted Germans might be expressed in another way by saying that they kept a less corrupted tradition of natural law than most other heathens; and I believe this would not involve any theological indiscretion. Indeed it might be a pious or at least an innocent speculation for an orthodox historian to surmise that herein they were special instruments of a dispensation outside or antecedent to the ordinary means of grace; the like assertion, at any rate, has constantly been made concerning the Roman Empire. It is embodied in the most striking manner by the legend of Trajan's miraculous translation to Paradise, the reward of a signal act of justice [1]; and this is the more notable when we remember that Trajan had authorized the persecution of Christians, though with reluctance. The same conception is the very groundwork of

---

[1] 'Qui fuerat iustus paganus factus est bonus christianus:' Benvenuto da Imola on Dante, Par. xx, *q.v.*, or any other good commentator.

Dante's treatise on Monarchy. Moreover we shall not forget that the Teutonic ideal has been exalted by writers who were good churchmen enough according to any test short of strict Roman orthodoxy, and in terms both stronger and wider than any that I have thought fit to use. But I do not call these champions in aid. It is not our business either to support or to contravene the Anglo-Saxon zeal of a Kemble, a Kingsley or a Freeman, when we can find everything we need for our particular purpose without going outside the text of Tacitus and the judicial caution of Gibbon's comment thereon. Perhaps it is needless to disclaim any such extravagant assertion as that the Angles and Saxons and Norsemen who settled in Britain were better men than their kinsfolk of the Continent. We know that they had the good fortune to settle on an island.

When we speak of the Germanic type and traditions as having persisted, we do not affirm that our remote forefathers' ideals of publicity, freedom, individual self-respect, and what else may be discoverable in our authorities or be fair matter of inference, have enjoyed an unbroken supremacy, still less a manifest one, throughout English history. There have always been adverse influences at work, and more than once they have seemed on the point of prevailing for good and all. Neither is it denied that there are reasonable and inevitable limits to the application of these ideals. Any civilized jurisprudence, for example, must pay some regard to the existence of State secrets which it would be dangerous to the common weal to disclose, and it must afford some protection to domestic and professional confidence; while it will not include in the name of personal freedom an unlimited franchise to defy the law and its officers, although there are people who behave as if it were so and even pretend to think so. The most we can expect is to find, as we do find, that the tradition of public life and common counsel has never been quite inoperative; that the rulers who have been most masterful in fact have been careful at least to respect it in form; and that open defiance of it has always been disastrous to those who ventured on such courses. The Tudors, by judicious use of methods which were on the whole formally correct (whatever historians or moralists may have to say to other aspects of them), gained far more real power than that which the Stuarts, often with quite a fair show of reasons on their side, lost by relying on the King's extraordinary privileges against Parliament and the common law. It is needless to repeat this familiar story, which I place among the things assumed to be sufficiently known.

Archaic virtues, like most good things in this world, are not without their drawbacks. Whatever else they are, they cannot help being archaic, and accordingly they go down to posterity clothed in antique and rigid forms. Those forms were once an effective and probably a necessary safeguard against a relapse into mere anarchy, the state of war in which every man's hand is against every other man's. But the rigidity which made them effectual for this purpose will make them, in a more settled order of things, an equally stubborn obstacle to improvement. Archaic justice binds the giants of primeval chaos in the fetters of inexorable word and form; and law, when she comes into her kingdom, must wage a new war to deliver herself from those very fetters. This conflict of substantial right and formalism is never exhausted; it is a perennial adventure of the Common Law, and perhaps the most arduous of all.

II. THE GIANTS AND THE GODS

At this day there is no need to explain that formality is an essential feature of archaic law. It has long ceased to be plausible, if it ever was, to regard strict insistence on form as a degeneration from some better pattern of justice which our remote ancestors were supposed to have followed in a simpler golden age. Persons who talk of primitive simplicity, if any still do, confound rudeness of instruments and poverty in execution with simplicity of ideas. Prehistoric language, customs and superstitions are exceedingly complex. If there was ever an earlier stage in which they were otherwise, we know nothing of it. The history of modern culture is, in essentials, a history of simplification.

Now formalism in law and procedure seems to have two roots, one rational and the other irrational. The rational ground is the need of a hard and fast rule to make it clear that the law is the same for all men. Suitors in the early age of regular justice are highly suspicious of personal favour and caprice, and will not hear of giving any room for discretion. As they apprehend it, a Court once allowed to relax the customary forms could make of the law itself whatever its members and managers for the time being pleased. The irrational ground goes back to the oldest form of superstition, older than both statecraft and priestcraft, the prehistoric belief.in symbolic magic. It is assumed that words have in themselves an operative virtue which is lost if any one word is substituted for any other. He who does not

14

follow the exact words prescribed by the legal ritual does
not bring himself within the law. If the Twelve Tables gave
an action for damage to 'trees' it would not do to say
'vines'; any such variation was to early Roman ears not
only futile but almost blasphemous. A medieval English
lawyer might have compromised on a *videlicet* and allowed
'certain trees of the plaintiff, to wit vines' to be well enough.
These two motives, jealousy of personal authority and superstitious worship of the letter, are as different as possible
in origin and nature, but they are by no means inconsistent.
Rather they have been a pair of hands to tie the magistrate
fast in bonds woven with the double strand of magic and
policy. Between them they have fostered, all the world
over, official and professional attachment to form for form's
sake, a passion with which we have all made acquaintance at
some time, to our greater or less vexation. Its operation is
not at all confined to legal proceedings. Neither of the
motives now mentioned will go very far towards accounting
for the actual origin of ceremonies and formulas. For that
purpose other causes would have to be discussed, and in
particular the taste or instinct which leads men to clothe
their collective action in dramatic and rhythmical shapes;
an instinct not without a practical side, as the symbols it
creates are both impressive at the time and easily remembered. Ritual of one sort and another answers to a desire
that lies pretty deep in human nature. But the further
analysis of this, whether simple or complex, would help us
very little just now. Certainly it would not explain why
legal forms, or any form, should be treated as invariable, for
that is by no means a universal attribute of ceremonies. It
is quite possible to have a type of ritual, even elaborate
ritual, with considerable room for variations; longer and

shorter alternative recensions, and so forth. It is no less possible to be strict in matters of detail without holding that a slip is fatal. Opinions differ as to the value of smartness in drill and equipment beyond what is positively needful, and some officers have been martinets. But surely no commander ever went so far as to tell his subalterns on the eve of going into action, that the battle would infallibly be lost, if a single button was awry. Therefore it seems to me that. we must not be tempted to dally with the aesthetic history of ritual at large. It is too remotely connected with our specific subject of legal formation, and we may leave anthropologists to settle its proper place and importance in their own learning.

There is an important distinction to be noted in the ways of early Germanic and probably of other procedure. It is not correct to say that everything was formal, but rather that, whenever form was required, no relaxation or amendment was admissible. When the members of the Court (originally the whole of the assembled free men) had the means of acting on their own immediate knowledge, they could act without any form at all. Thus, in criminal justice, the manslayer who was pursued and caught red-handed was put to death without ceremony: this was so in England down to the thirteenth century. Thus, in civil matters, it seems the county court could itself bear witness to a disposition made by a landholder whose right to make it was admitted, and then give judgment accordingly.[1] Let the fact be disputed, however, and our ancestors' minds were at once filled with deep distrust of human testimony and entire disbelief in the power of human judgment to discover the truth, perhaps also in the existence of any impartial will

[1] Kemble, Cod. Dipl. DCCLV; Essays in Anglo-Saxon Law, p. 365.

to discover it. An external standard was demanded, but not in the rational sense in which my friend Justice Holmes has taught us to use the term. In this manner we find that formalism is at its strongest in archaic methods of proof, while executive acts, partly but not altogether by the necessary reason of their nature, are to a great extent exempt from it.

Now as to proof, the archaic view of it is quite simple. I do not say evidence, because there are no archaic rules of evidence; the conception is unknown. Evidence is offered with a view to leading a judge or a jury to some inference of fact which may determine or help to determine the decision of the case as a whole. But the archaic proof comes after judgment, not before. It is adjudged that John or Peter is to make his proof. Not that he is bound to make it, as a modern student is tempted to think, but that he is entitled to make it, that he has the prerogative of proving as they said in comparatively modern Scottish practice. Formal affirmation by the plaintiff generally reinforced by a 'suit' of fellow-swearers, has been the first step. It has been met by denial, a formal denial which, on pain of failure, had to traverse every point of the plaintiff's assertion word for word. The Court awards proof to one or the other party, and then he is in possession of the cause. Let us suppose that the proof is by oath, which is the most regular and instructive case. There is a process by which the adversary can stop the oath if he will, at his peril, challenge the swearer and his helpers as incredible. He may seize the hand before it is uplifted to swear, or before it touches the relics on which the oath is to be made; he may bar the way into the church by stretching his arm or his sword across the door. Herein, as in all steps of archaic procedure, he acts, at best, at his

c

own risk, But he must act at exactly the right moment.
The oath, once begun, may not be interrupted.   Every one
who has seen the 'Götterdämmerung' will remember Brünnhilde's attempt to 'levy' Siegfried from his oath, not before
he swears but after he has sworn.   Wagner took no more
license than many other dramatists have taken, surely none
so great as the wholesale violation of natural as well as legal
justice which is accepted without demur — such is Shakespeare's art, in the suit of Shylock against Antonio.   No
one is troubled there by a civil action being turned without
notice into an official prosecution of the plaintiff for an of-
fence of which no one has accused him ; and in the 'Götterdämmerung' nobody minds Brünnhilde's interruption being
out of time.   But I fear the only possible judgment of
Gunther's court, off the stage, would have been that the
proceeding was altogether irregular.   Siegfried's 'prerogative of proving' should have been challenged before he
could speak a word.

, On the other hand, the oath-taker and his helpers, when
they have begun, must perform their parts exactly, not only
in word, but in gesture.   A hand held up must not be lowered,
a hand laid on relics, or on a sword, or on the oath helpers'
hands, must not be moved until the oath is fully spoken.[1]
If nothing goes wrong in the solemnity, if all the right words
are said in the right order, if all hands and fingers keep their
right station, and if, all being duly done, the customary
pause has elapsed without any one being visibly smitten by
the divine wrath for perjury, then the proof is not only complete but conclusive. .

---

[1] Brunner. D. R. G. ii. 433, and Forschungen zur Gesch. des deutschen u.
franzōs. Rechts, 385, 386.   In some French custumals rules of this kind are
recorded as still in force, with only slight relaxations, in the late fifteenth century, as appears from the passage last cited.

What has been said about proof not being a burden but an advantage does not apply to trial by battle, nor to the other kinds of 'judgment of God,' namely ordeal by fire or water. In the case of battle, the parties have an equal chance. As for the man sent to the ordeal, he is already half condemned; if he were of good repute he would have claimed, and would have been allowed, to clear himself by oath. What he gets is a last chance of escape, and a better one, apparently, than most moderns would guess. Offers to prove claims by any form of ordeal, 'omnibus modis' or 'omnibus legibus,' may be found, no doubt, from Domesday Book onwards. I have never met with any case of such an offer ripening into performance, and I strongly suspect that they were not seriously meant or taken.

Neither ordeal nor trial by battle could be reduced to strictly ceremonial proceedings. And yet it is abundantly clear that trial by battle in civil cases did from an early time tend to become little more than a picturesque setting for an ultimate compromise. The parties agree at the last moment; the judges call on the champions to strike a blow or two, 'the King's strokes,' for sport; the 'horned staves' — representing, it seems, the Frankish double ax — resound on the targets; the shaven and leather-coated professionals depart lovingly, we may presume, to drink up a competent portion of their fees; and the public, we hope, think the show was good enough without any slaying or hanging. Also we read of much incidental and preliminary ceremony: the champion's gloves are offered to the Court with a silver penny in every finger, and, contrary to the intention of preventing perjury, which was originally given as the reason for the judicial duel, there is elaborate swearing. But it does not appear that every detail was essential, or that the whole thing would have come to naught if, for example, only four pennies had been found in one of the gloves. In fact, the medieval writings in which the ritual of the judicial combat has been described at various times are pretty strong to show that at none of those times was the proceeding common enough to be fresh in any one's memory. Perhaps even in the fourteenth century, certainly in the sixteenth, it was an antiquarian pageant in which little mistakes were very possible. On the last occasion when battle was waged, in the early ninteenth century,[1] a fearfully and wonderfully adorned glove, supposed to be of medieval pattern, was thrown down in Court. It was remarkable for having no fingers at all,[2] which would have been incorrect in a writ of right, but some one may have thought it was the proper practice in an appeal of felony. Long before this, however, the picturesque aspect of the ceremony had prevailed over the real archaic faith which takes adherence to every point of form in dead earnest. There is already something consciously romantic about the latter generations of the Middle Ages. Perhaps this was not the least fatal symptom of decay.

Such were the strange guardians among whom our lady the Common Law was born and cradled. For they were true guardians in their day. Caprice, even well meant and at

---

[1] The well known case of Ashford v. Thornton, see Stephen, Hist. Cr. Law, i. 249. It is perhaps a superfluous precaution to remind the reader that there was no battle; the appellant hoped to persuade the court that the case was so clear against the appellee as to deprive him of the right to 'defend the same with his body.'

[2] Neilson, Trial by Combat, 329. All the authorities on the subject, I believe, are collected in this excellent book. A note of the ceremonies made in 1346 was edited by Mr. Pike, among other unprinted cases, in 1908: Y.B. 20 Ed. III (Rolls series), p. 483. A still earlier one (1330) was printed by Dugdale, Orig. Jurid. 68, from a Lincoln's Inn Ms. The fact that a minute report was thought worth making at those dates is significant.

times, as it might chance, well doing caprice, had to be kept
at arm's length at all costs.   Better even bad rules than a
rule which is not of law.   It was a great and a true word that
Jhering spoke when he said: 'Form is the sworn foe of
caprice, she is Freedom's twin sister.' [1]   The giants of the
prime are stark and grim figures in our sight, yet their force
cleared a way for the Gods through chaos, and without them
the Gods would never have come to Valhalla.   But the
guardians became tyrants when, in a community growing
civilized, the judicial results of a semi-magical ritual ceased
to be tolerable, and the so-called judgments of God were
openly deemed unjust alike by men of war and by men of
religion.   Their ways could not be mended; they must be
broken, and a new body must be fashioned for the justice
which in its old embodiment was too visibly blind even in
the eyes of twelfth century suitors.   The masters who were
no longer protectors but oppressors must be fought with
and overthrown if the law were to be made an organ of living
righteousness.   Truly the spirit of our infant laws had need
of a mighty champion.   It was written of the Church that
kings should be her nursing fathers.   No less truly might it
be said of the Common Law.   The king's overriding power,
a power both to devise and to execute, was the only one
strong enough for the work.   Royal inquests, royal precepts and decisions, ingenuity of royal officers at least as
eager to bring fees into the king's coffers and enhance the
reputation of the king's court as to procure ease and satisfaction to suitors, were the means, not precisely of abolishing
the inflexible and cumbrous old procedure — we had not
formally begun to abolish anything — but of relegating it to
an obscurity where it was speedily forgotten, and so com-

[1] Geist des röm. Rechts, ii, 471, 4th ed., 1883.

pletely forgotten too that professed antiquarian lawyers could, almost down to our own time, believe trial by jury to be immemorial. Indeed, we should be speaking almost literal truth if we said that our lady the Common Law never had much trouble with the forms of archaic proof. By the time she had got to serious work they were hardly more dangerous than Giant Pagan. Proof by oath lingered through the Middle Ages, and much later, in the wager of law, but in so many ways hampered and discouraged that it is already something of a curiosity in the sixteenth century. Monsters of this brood are, at a modern lawyer's first sight, clumsy lubber fiends from whom there is not even the sport of a good fight to be had. The real danger was more insidious. The ancient rigid formalism was dead but not exorcised, and the ghost of it walked, in some jurisdictions it still walks, disguising itself under more or less plausible reasons of logic or expediency. Without letting ourselves be too much entangled in the maze of technical details, let us now see how this came about.

Whatever we may think of the king's new justice, as it stood between six and seven centuries ago, comparing it with all that we have learnt and accomplished since, there is no doubt that it was immensely more rational than the prehistoric methods it supplanted, or that its rapid success was due to its merits. The king did not want to make it cheap; it had to support itself and be a source of revenue. It was not to be had at all times or at all places; the commissioners of assize carried it round the country, but at considerable intervals. As for the older visitations of itinerant justices, the justices in eyre as they were called, they were quite as much bent on collecting fines, and discovering the irregularities which bred them, as on improving the administration of the law. Their appearance was certainly not welcome in the latter days of the thirteenth century, if it ever had been; and in the course of the fourteenth century the cumbrous machinery of the eyre was wholly superseded by the more convenient jurisdiction of the justices of assize. Otherwise no special pains were taken to make the king's courts easy of access or attractive, though there are indications that the king's judges had the deliberate purpose of keeping the old popular courts in a lower place. When we speak of their jurisdiction and methods as supplanting those of the county court, it must not be understood that the process was sudden, or was ever logically completed. Our lady the Common Law is not like a tidy French housewife whose broom sweeps out all the corners; one doubts whether she ever will be. Remnants of archaism, wager of law and such like, hung about the older forms of action. Still the characteristic merits of the king's justice were great, and its own. So far as' it had a free hand, it did not charge men with crimes on suspicion and drive them to clear themselves, if they could, by absurd and precarious tests. It did not decide civil controversies by counting oaths or by competition in exact knowledge of verbal formulas. It did make some serious attempt: at ascertaining facts and applying intelligible rules of law to the facts of which the Court was possessed by admission or proof. Pleading in civil actions, down to the fourteenth century, was already a game of skill, but it was played by living discussion before the judges, who acted as moderators and directors. It ended, not in a judgment, but in a preliminary settlement of the points at issue. To understand the necessary limitations and the real merit of the system, we must remember that the king's Court did not profess to have universal jurisdiction. It provided certain remedies in

certain cases in which the king thought worthy of his interference. The plaintiff had to show the Court how the facts
he alleged brought him within some species of justice it professed to do. He could not tell his story at large and leave the
Court to find, with or without the aid of advocacy, what law
was applicable. A dialectic process of some kind was necessary to fix the point for adjudication, and to guide the
future practice of the professional counsellors who were now
becoming the servants of the law. This creative dialectic,
working on a still fresh and plastic material, is what we find
in the earlier Year Books; not official or formal records (as
we now know, thanks to Maitland, and as at least one American scholar suspected before), but notes of young lawyers
keen on learning their business, and eager to make sure how
far they could venture to be ingenious without rashness.
They cared very little who the parties were, and less about
the end of the case. Good pleading was their ambition; the
art which commanded the approval of the Court and the
confidence of clients, and might lead them one day to be
serjeants themselves, canvassing points familiarly with the
judges, and bring a fortunate few of them even to the Bench.
When the semi-official talking in any cause in the Common
Pleas was done, the students knew pretty well what was
sound pleading in the general opinion of the judges and
serjeants. To be sure, some counsel were more obstinate
in their own views than others. In the very latest days of
oral pleading counsel might say to the Court, thinking his
adversary had not the courage of his invention: Surely he
will never dare to put that on the record ! But in this case
the Court promptly said it was well enough, and enrolled it
on the spot.[1] What goes on the record after discussion is

---

[1] 42 Ed. III, 4, pl. 14 *ad fin.* (the text as printed is not free from difficulty).

understood to be informally passed as good. Only the
graver doubts are set down as matter for solemn decision.
Then we have meetings of all the judges at which they argue
with counsel and with one another, take new points, throw
out hints and warnings for the benefit of juniors, with all
the zest of their earlier days in the profession. It was a
highly technical affair, no doubt. Medieval lawyers and
probably medieval laymen would have been shocked at the
suggestion that it could be anything else. But the system
was very far from being a hide-bound formalism. It was
spoilt by abuse of its own power of free and varied development.

Technical dialectic is an excellent servant; the lay people
may talk as they please, after their own 'talent' as the
Year Books say, but every lawyer who has sat on committees
knows that untrained amateur pedantry can be both more
absurd and more unjust than any professional bias. Nevertheless good servants often want to be masters, and make
very bad masters when they get their way. So it happened
with common-law pleading and procedure. The mischief
cannot be ascribed in any great measure to the partial
survivals of extreme archaism. Those curiosities, as they
occur in relatively modern law-books, have received quite
as much attention as they deserve for any purpose except
that of pure archæology. Various devices kept them within
bounds which made them practically harmless. It is true
that this was not done without paying a price for it, but that
is not the subject immediately before us. On the whole,
what little was left of the genuine ancient formalism caused
less inconvenience than might have been expected. But the
old spirit of it was scotched, not killed, and the ghost fell
to work, with only too much success, to effect a lodgment in

the new body. John Bunyan made a pretty bad mistake when he represented Giant Pope as decrepit; if he could have looked outside England he would have seen the counter-reformation making its conquests. Probably Henry of Bratton, perhaps even Glanvill or the learned clerk who wrote under the shield of his name, was sanguine enough to hope that no man would dare to make new rubbish-heaps where once the king's broom had swept. If so, they were mistaken in the same sort. The new material itself was attacked by a parasitic growth of later medieval exuberance. Form for form's sake had been a stern mistress; the demon of subtilty for subtilty's sake was an alluring siren. Her charms might not allure us very much; they were fatal to scholars whose intellectual habits were in many ways like those of a clever schoolboy. The tendency to useless refinement is apparent even during the time of oral pleading; but the fatal step was the change from open discussion in Court to the delivery of written pleadings between the parties without any judicial control. Future editors of the later Year Books will probably be able to clear up various details. The main points of the story, however, have long been well known.[1] Inasmuch as this newer formalism was not honestly archaic but must rather be classed, from an artist's point of view, as a product of flamboyant archaistic decadence, we need not feel bound to treat it with any respect.

---

[1] They were set forth in the early nineteenth century in an excellent book which is perhaps more honoured at this day in America than in the mother land, Stephen on Pleading. Fuller confirmation has been added by later scholars, such as (to speak only of my own countrymen) Maitland, Mr. Pike, and Dr. Holdsworth; all of them accept Stephen's account as correct in essentials.

III. SURREBUTTER CASTLE

PERVERSE ingenuity, once let loose on the art of pleading, went for some centuries from bad to worse, notwithstanding occasional mitigations. It would be tedious, and for our purpose useless, to follow the history of corruption and confusion in detail. Enough to say that the older forms of action remained comparatively simple but stiff and cumbrous, while the newer ones were elastic, but tricky because the limits of their elasticity were uncertain. The system was not even logical, for a strictly logical adherence to consequences would have brought the business of the Courts to a dead-lock; and the partial remedies applied by legislation, or by forensic and in some cases judicial ingenuity, did not even pretend to be consistent with any systematic doctrine at all. In many cases there were alternative forms of procedure having different incidents wholly unconnected with the substance of the case; while in others, again for no intelligible reason, there was none, and moreover it was often difficult to be sure what the proper form of action was.[1]

We may now proceed to see what the bastard formalism of pleading had come to in England in the second quarter of the nineteenth century, and we may use the guidance of a very learned person, Serjeant Hayes,[2] afterwards a justice of the Queen's Bench for a short time, who knew the system thor-

[1] The learned reader may see a few examples collected in a footnote, Pollock on Torts, 8th ed., 231.

[2] George Hayes, 1805–1869; called to the Bar 1830, Serjeant 1856, Justice, 1868.

27

oughly and did his best to bring about its downfall. The
work to which I invite the attention of any learned friends
not yet acquainted with it (making no apology to those who
are, for they will require none) was written by Hayes, while
he was still a junior, about 1850. It is entitled 'Crogate's
Case : a dialogue in the Shades on Special Pleading Reform.'[1]
One of the interlocutors is Baron Surrebutter, a transparent
disguise for Baron Parke, or rather that half of him which
was devoted to the technical side of process and pleading.
He was transferred to the House of Lords as Lord Wens-
leydale a few years after the drastic reformation, by the
Common Law Procedure Act of 1852, of the system he had
so zealously maintained in the Court of Exchequer. I do
not know that he made any great show of mourning for it
when the thing was done; certainly the catastrophe did not
shorten his life, for he was eighty-five years old when he died
in 1868, a date within the professional memory of men still
active on the bench and at the bar. When there was not
any point of pleading before the Court, no man could handle
matters of principle with greater clearness or broader common
sense. The other personage is 'the celebrated Crogate,
who in his mortal state gave rise to the great case reported in
8 Co. 66, and whose name is inseparably connected with the
doctrine of *de injuria*.' As that doctrine is not intelligible
without some detailed acquaintance with the forms of common law pleading, and has been obsolete for more than half
a century alike in England and in New York, I shall merely
observe that any one desiring an explanation of it may
readily be satisfied in the adjacent State of New Jersey,

[1] Privately printed, London, 1854, and privately reprinted 1892, together
with other writings of Hayes, in a volume entitled Hayesiana. In the reprint
there are divers minute typographical variations from the original; but they
do not deserve to be enumerated by even the most minute bibliographer.

where, if I am not mistaken, the replication *de injuria* is in full force to this day. Enough to remind the student that Crogate, being plaintiff in an action of trespass, replied *de injuria* to a special plea which he ought to have answered in some other way (let our learned friends in New Jersey tell us how, if they will); and that, as the Dialogue shows more at large, an attempted reform of pleading in England by the New Rules of 1834 led to an outbreak of new technicalities including an active revival of this particular form, which had become almost obsolete.

The shade of the learned Baron newly arrived in Hades complains to Crogate of his treatment by the court of Rhadamanthus, a court below, but from which, to the Baron's indignation, error does not lie. He has deceived the vigilance of Cerberus, 'whose multifarious head' he says, 'struck me as being decidedly bad on special demurrer. I had, however, fortunately prepared myself against this danger by bringing with me a very special traverse, which I immediately threw out to him as a bait. He greedily caught it and swallowed the inducement in a twinkling; but the *absque hoc* stuck in his throat and nearly choked him, and in the meantime I made my escape.' Before Rhadamanthus, Baron Surrebutter relates, he was charged with having obstructed justice with the frivolous technicalities of special pleading. 'I pleaded that special pleading was a wise and useful system, and that I had helped to remedy all its defects by the New Rules. This plea was perhaps bad in form, as an argumentative general issue; but I was willing to run the risk of a special demurrer for the chance of entrapping my opponent into a denial of only one branch of my plea. . . . But he replied by asserting that special pleading was an abominable system, and that I had made it much worse

by the New Rules.   To the replication I demurred specially
on the ground of duplicity; but to my astonishment the
Court, on my refusing to withdraw my demurrer, most
unceremoniously set it aside as frivolous, and gave judgment
against me.'   And so Baron Surrebutter finds himself in a
whimsical limbo of pleaders and litigants, where former
masters of the art are engaged in an interminable exchange
of special pleadings, or attempting to frame undemurrable
defences in actions brought under the New Rules.

The main part of the Dialogue consists of the learned
Baron's hopeless endeavours to make Mr. Crogate understand
the necessity and elegance of the decision in his case.   Inci-
dentally he explains how the amount of special pleading
varies with the form of action.   'The forms of pleading are
more or less strict, according to the nature of the action;
and in many actions there is, in substance, no special pleading at all.   In actions on *contracts*, if the facts are such as to
render it necessary, according to the established rules of the
court, to declare specially, great strictness and particularity
are enforced, and the simplest questions are often involved
in much complication of pleading; but if the case admits
of the use of certain general or common counts (which indeed are applicable in the great majority of ordinary actions)
the whole matter is left pretty much at large, and the most
complicated questions are tried on simplest statements.
So in actions on *torts*, you may have more or less special
pleading, entirely according to the form of action which you
elect, or are obliged to adopt.   Thus, if your goods are taken
away, and you sue the wrong-doer in *trespass* (as you did in
your own case, Mr. Crogate) you will have special pleading
in all its strictness; but if you choose to sue in *trover*, and
make a fictitious statement that you casually lost your goods,

and that the defendant found and converted them; here he is allowed to deny the fictitious loss and finding, and may set up almost any possible defense, under a denial of the alleged ownership and conversion of the goods; or if you prefer to sue in *detinue*, and state a fictitious delivery or bailment of the goods to the defendant (which fiction he is not allowed to deny), you will have rather more special pleading than in *trover*, but considerably less than in *trespass*. If you are assaulted and beaten, you cannot escape special pleading by any fictitious allegation, but you are obliged to sue in *trespass*, and the defendant to justify specially. If you sue for a *trespass* to your land, however small the injury, the greatest strictness of pleading is required, but if you are actually turned out, you may recover the land itself by a fictitious mode of proceeding called *ejectment*, without any special pleading at all.' So did an accomplished master of the so-called science of pleading state the results attained after several centuries of elaboration. The irony of Hayes's dialogue is completed by Baron Surrebutter's account of the new-fangled county courts.[1] It seems well to give this without abridgment, preserving Crogate's part.

'*Crog.* Well, well, Mr. Judge, I see how the whole thing stands pretty clearly. The more you patch and mend a bad thing the worse you make it; and this is just what you have been doing by your New Rules. But what I want to know is, whether there are no courts where you can get justice, or something like it, without any special pleading?

Sur. B. Oh, yes. In consequence of an idle and absurd clamour on the part of the public, some inferior courts were

---

[1] Established in 1847. They are not in any way connected with the ancient county court. Their jurisdiction has been much extended in our own time,

established a short time back to enable the common people to sue for small debts and damages under *twenty* pounds; and in these courts, the proceedings are wholly free from the refinements of special pleading.

Crog. But, if special pleading is a good thing, why is it done without in these courts?

Sur. B. Because of the expense and delay which the forms of correct pleading would occasion, and because neither practitioners nor judges could be expected to understand the system properly; and moreover, Mr. Crogate, in these trifling matters the greatest object is to administer substantial justice [1] in the simplest form and at the least expense.

Crog. Well, in my ignorance, I should have thought that would have been the object in great cases as well as small. But, pray, what mode of proceeding do you use instead of special pleading?

Sur. B. The simplest process in the world. The forms of action have been practically abolished. The plaintiff gives a concise statement or notice of his claim, and the defendant of his defense (where it is considered proper that he should do so) in plain English, unfettered by the technical rules of pleading. If either party really stands in need of further information, the judge requires it to be given; or if either party complains of surprise, and requires further time, he adjourns the trial upon just terms. The case being

---

[1] But in Hayes's own preface there is a note on 'substantial justice' which must not be overlooked. 'A good specimen of this favourite commodity is furnished in the following well-known decision. A defendant having alleged his inability to pay the plaintiff's demand, the plaintiff admitted it, but maintained that though the defendant himself could not pay, he had an aunt who could; and the judge, being of this opinion, made an order against the aunt. This is said to be a leading county court authority, and is commonly cited as " My Aunt's Case."'

understood and ready for trial, he decides it, and there is an end of the matter.

Crog. And does this answer?

Sur. B. It has not been complained of. In fact, suitors were so well satisfied with these new-fangled courts that they were anxious to go to them in cases which ought to have come to us . . . and it remains to be seen whether the effect will not be to transfer to them the great bulk of the civil business of the country, and to leave the Superior Courts without employment; a result which will be obviously fatal to the law of England.'

Baron Surrebutter then offers to give a classified exposition of the doctrine, considering, 'First, when *de injuria* may clearly be replied. Secondly, when it clearly cannot be replied. Thirdly, when it is probable that it may be replied. Fourthly, when it is probable it cannot be replied. And, fifthly, when it is altogether doubtful whether it can or cannot be replied.' But he does not get very far, for Crogate pays no attention to the exquisite distinctions reported in Meeson and Welsby, and runs away 'in great anguish of mind'; and so ends the Dialogue. In a final soliloquy the Baron announces his intention of seeking out the learned Serjeant Williams, the editor of Saunders' Reports, to discuss the high and dubious question whether a *virtute cujus* is traversable.

It must appear strange to a plain man that the evils of artificial pleading were felt a century before Hayes wrote, and some attempt was made to remedy them: an attempt of which Blackstone tells us for the credit of enlightened eighteenth-century practice as he knew it, but in words including some express apology and much implied admission. 'Formerly the general issue was seldom pleaded, except when the

D

party meant wholly to deny the charge alleged against him.
. . . But the science of special pleading having been frequently perverted to the purposes of chicane and delay, the
courts have, of late, in some instances, and the legislature in
many more, permitted the general issue to be pleaded, which
leaves everything open, the fact, the law, and the equity of
the case.' He adds that 'so great a relaxation of the
strictness anciently observed' has not been found to lead to
confusion in practice.[1] So far well; but when Blackstone
spoke of the Courts having improved matters 'in some
instances, and the legislature in many more,' he was unconsciously pointing to a new source of trouble shortly to come.
Our ancestors of the eighteenth century were not stupid or
slothful. They knew the raiment of the law wanted mending, and they mended it as well as they could in their time,
having also campaigns in Flanders and Jacobite rebellions
to think of. But it was only patchwork, and ultimately the
rents were made worse. After the common fashion of
English public business, reforms were introduced piecemeal
and without any settled plan, and so, while they lightened
some of the most pressing grievances, they raised fresh difficulties, almost at every turn; and in the first half of the
nineteenth century the confusion of common law pleading
had become, as Serjeant Hayes found it, more intricate than
ever. I have not heard that in any American jurisdiction
there was any judicial or other regulation whose effects were
as disastrous as those of the New Rules made by the English
judges in 1834; but I suppose that on the whole complaints of
the same kind were pretty common, as otherwise it would be
hard to account for the existence of modern codes of procedure in this and other States, and for various alterations short

[1] Bl. Comm. iii. 305, 306.

of actual code pleading, from the simple and almost patriarchal method of Vermont, which Mr. Phelps described to
me many years ago, to the more elaborate scheme of Massachusetts, resembling in a general way that which satisfied
our courts in England, under the Common Law Procedure
Acts, from 1852[1] to 1875.

There is nothing to be said here about the other systems
which coexisted with common law procedure in England
down to our own time, and still have an independent existence
in some jurisdictions. It is doubtful whether in any case the
practitioners at Westminster could have learnt much from
them; for they started from a wholly different and much more
ambitious conception of the Court's office, namely that it
had the duty or at least the power of finding out the truth of
the matter for itself. At any rate there is nothing to show
substantial influence in fact from those quarters, as distinct
from the stock of learning and intellectual habit which was
common to all educated persons in the Middle Ages. Our
lady the Common Law did not reign alone, but her diplomatic relations with her consorts or rivals, whichever they
should be called, were of the scantiest. The common law
treatises on pleading, down to Stephen inclusive, do not so
much as mention the Courts of Chancery or Admiralty.
So far as there was any influence it was the other way, and
in the case of equity procedure not with the happiest results.
Indeed, the vices of subtilty and prolixity found at least as
easy subjects of temptation in the Chancery and the civilian
jurisdictions as elsewhere. By working on the quite sincere
desire of those Courts to do perfect justice to all parties and

[1] The Massachusetts reform was of nearly the same date. I should not
think it likely that the American and English draftsmen had any communi-
cation or knowledge of each other's work.

interests, they were able to present themselves in a specious guise; and they revelled in pleadings of enormous length and interminable verbal repetitions which had not even the merit of leading to the statement of any definite question for decision.

There was just one genuine archaic element that persisted in the decadent forms of common law pleading: the imperious desire for an authoritative decision of some kind rather than the best or the most complete solution. Somehow the parties must be driven to categorical contradiction on some single question of fact or law. Down to the latest period of unreformed pleading this was declared to be a fundamental principle, and we have no right to doubt that, being repeated by so many sages of the law, the declaration was made with perfect sincerity. Those learned persons might have known, if they had ever considered the matter with their eyes open, that their ideal was incompatible with any practical handling of modern disputes arising out of modern affairs. Perhaps it would be too much to expect a Baron Surrebutter to stand apart from the technical point of view to which he was bred. But at all events he could not help knowing that as often as not the apparent singleness of the final issue was merely formal. A short and comprehensive denial of the plaintiff's claim to fulfilment of duty or redress of wrong, a plea of Non Assumpsit or Not Guilty, might raise multifarious controversies of both law and fact, to be left 'at large' to a jury. Such cases were not abnormal; on the contrary, they were very common, probably a great majority. Loose issues of that sort being exactly what the theory professed to regard as shocking, it is hardly too much to say that its principles were outraged every day. The defendant who elected to rely on one special ground had to be very careful; but he who elected to deny the plaintiff's claim in the lump and take his chance on the evidence merely said, in effect: 'I admit nothing and wait to see what you can make of it.' We need not add, except for very innocent learners, that the party's advisers made the choice, in every case where it was open, according to his interest as it appeared to them, and not with any further regard for the symmetry or congruity of their art. The truth is that a severely logical application of the assumed principles of pleading would have been intolerable even to a generation of formalists, but nobody had the courage to say so. With such content as we may, we must even believe that our lady the Common Law, like many other good-natured people busied with more matters than they can attend to in person, allowed herself to be put upon and her customers harassed by fussy, greedy and sometimes dishonest underlings. The warning is not out of date.

IV. ENEMIES IN THE GATE

So far we have spoken of dangers to the Common Law within her own household. Before we can understand the limits and the difficulties of possible remedies in the Middle Ages and even later, we must consider the perpetual conflict with external foes which had to be waged at the same time. One kind of these, as they were the most shameless, were the most formidable, namely men who were strong enough, in parts of England remote from the central authority, to defy legal justice and legal process openly. Nowadays we do not easily realize the chronic persistence of such behaviour in a land whose rulers are seriously minded to keep order. Riot is not impossible in the most civilized of jurisdictions, but it is abnormal; it is at most an occasional scandal. Powerful interests may be arrayed against the law; they may dispose of great resources and be capable of giving much trouble. But they have at any rate to do the law of the land some kind of lip-service. Their aim is, if possible, to capture its machinery and use it for their own purposes. Chicane and corruption are their weapons, and the corruption is seldom undisguised even when it is notorious. Intimidation is employed more sparingly, not from any moral scruple, but because it is less profitable and provokes defensive combination; and when it is employed, it is in the form of social and pecuniary pressure. Violence is avoided as impolitic, unless there is a fair chance of representing it as lawful self-help. A very different state of things prevailed in England down to

the sixteenth century. We find the danger of great men
defying the law not only recognized but prominent in the
dooms of Anglo-Saxon kings. As the extent and effective-
ness of royal justice increase after the Norman Conquest
we still find repeated and anxious condemnation of those who
take the law into their own hands. Whoever asserts his
right without due process of law puts himself in the wrong:
iniuste quia sine iudicio. The principle is carried even to
greater lengths than our modern law finds necessary.
Whether we look at the common law of disseisin or the
statutes against forcible entry, we find the same continuous
protest, expressing a real and arduous conflict with lawlessness. Neither must we suppose that the law was always
gaining ground. Under a strong king much crime went
undiscovered and unpunished, police methods being rudimentary; but private war was repressed. Nevertheless
the elements of revolt were still there and ready to break out
at the first sign of weakness. The middle quarters of the
fifteenth century were a period of reactionary disorder of
which our strictly legal authorities disclose very little. England was delivered over, one might almost say, to the great
faction fight called the Wars of the Roses, and to innumer-
able smaller feuds of private greed and ambition. Every
man who had property worth protecting was as much compelled to secure the protection of some great lord as if the
feudal structure of society had relapsed into its crudest
Merovingian infancy. Forcible disseisin was rife, statutory
penalties notwithstanding, and was often planned and exe-
cuted as a military operation. Country gentlemen's houses
were fortified, attacked and defended 'with strong hand in
manner of war,' and the fortunate possessors of firearms
improvised loopholes cunningly placed too low to be used for

archery in case of a hostile occupation. It is true that the process of law was not formally arrested, but corruption and intimidation of juries, besides the simpler method of packing the jury from the first, were so common that no man would embark on a lawsuit without powerful influence at his back. 'God send us a good sheriff this year' may seem a pious and innocent wish, but in the mouth of a faithful steward, when the balance was trembling between Lancaster and York, a good sheriff meant one who could be trusted to impanel the right sort of jury for the steward's lord.[1] All this may be learnt, in abundant quantity and variety, from the contemporary and practical evidence of the Paston Letters. The factions of York and Lancaster both acted under colour of legal claims to the crown, on which Fortescue and others expended much dialectic ingenuity. But this can hardly be taken as evidence of any specially English show of respect for law, or desire to have the law on one's side. It is a common feature of all political controversy in the Middle Ages. All it does prove, if proof were needed, is that the aim of each party was not an anarchical conquest or a social revolution, but to acquire control of the established governmental machine as a going concern, using for that purpose, without legal or moral scruple, as much force as it could command.

These facts must be borne in mind if we would understand the rapid development of extraordinary jurisdictions under the Tudor dynasty. Lack of executive power had always been the weak point of the Common Law, and in order to

[1] Paston Letters, No. 420 (ii, 59, 60, ed. 1896). This bailiff was himself under a charge of felony, and laments that the trial was postponed when he 'was through with the scheryff and panel made after myn avice.' Mr. C. Plummer's introduction to Fortescue on the Governance of England, Oxford, 1885, gives a good summary view of the time.

keep faction permanently repressed, after Henry VII's victory had closed the dynastic strife, more drastic methods were required. What the Chancellor was already doing in matters of private law was now to be done by the King's Council in the Star Chamber and in the special palatine and frontier jurisdictions. Thus Sir Thomas Smith tells us of 'the insolency of the noblemen and gentlemen of the north part of England, who being far from the king and the seat of justice made almost as it were an ordinary war among themselves'; and Bacon speaks in like manner of 'maintenance or headship of great persons' as one chief reason why jurisdiction of this kind was needful and politic; and we could have no two more competent witnesses to the traditions of sixteenth-century statecraft. More than this, there was a time when the demand for strong government was virtually leagued against the Common Law with a learned intellectual movement among Romanizing scholars and publicists. Maitland has given us the proofs in his brilliant essay — not the less solid because brilliant — on English Law and the Renaissance. Towards the middle of the century, the situation might well have seemed critical; a foreign observer might even have expected that the Court of Chancery, not yet officially declared to be an ordinary court of justice, would easily be drawn into the confederacy. Such a forecast would have been wrong but not without plausibility. What actually followed we know; the last quarter of the sixteenth century saw, concurrently with the steady growth of equity jurisdiction, a great revival of the Courts at Westminster, based on clear and proud consciousness of their historical authority and doctrine. Antiquarian jurisprudence was militant and triumphant, with the compilers of the Abridgments and the printers of the Year Books for its armourers, and Sir Edward Coke for its champion; . a champion to be venerated, still active and valiant, by a younger generation fighting the battle of constitutional right with like weapons against Charles I. The history was not always critical in either case, but that was not material for the result. Such a revival is among the most impressive evidences of a vitality not only professional but national, which might be obscured but could not be suppressed by adverse conjunctures.

Yet, when all is said, our lady the Common Law had to abide a season of some danger and much disparagement; and whatever tends to disparage the Common Law must in the same measure encourage all kinds of encroachment, and especially the official kind. Not that England can be said to have suffered from excess of officials or administration, in secular affairs at any rate, at any time before the classical framework of the Common Law was finally settled. In common frankness it must be admitted that in the sixteenth century, while the executive had nominally very large powers, its instruments for ordinary occasions were both weak and scanty. One way and another a great deal of officialism had to be created if the conditions of life were to be tolerable for lawful men. But the Tudor sovereigns and their ministers were easily tempted to provide it in arbitrary ways. Hence arose high prerogative doctrines, claims to legislate in minor matters by proclamation, and other controversial pretensions which ultimately filled the cup of the Stuarts to overflowing. Charles II, alone of his dynasty, had a share of the practical worldly wisdom that told the Tudors where to hold their hand. In modern England the problem of reconciling administrative efficiency with the principles of lawful authority has been solved by recourse to the legal omnipotence of Parliament, a Parliament representing the will of the people in a very different fashion from its predecessors three centuries ago. When we remember that the venerable institution of justices of the peace is itself statutory, there seems to be very little risk in saying that all executive acts of importance (in domestic affairs at any rate) are now done under statutory authority of one sort or another. But Parliament is not always vigilant, and the Ministers who frame statutes are advised by permanent officials in technical matters. Thus there is an ever growing tendency, constitutional traditions and safeguards notwithstanding, to confer more and more discretion, often of a substantially judicial kind, on officials of the great departments of state who practically cannot be made responsible. Of late years there have been many protests, quite irrespective of party politics; indeed the zeal of either party to use encroachment of legislation on ordinary legal jurisdiction as a topic against the other is naturally tempered by the reflection that the accusing party has itself made statutes of that kind by the score, and will want to make them again when it comes back to office. A similar tendency in American State legislation was noted by my learned friend Mr. St. George Tucker of Virginia when he presided over the American Bar Association some years ago. The ravages of the gipsy moth and the brown-tailed moth have been the cause, it seems, of administrative enactments in Massachusetts which perhaps only strict necessity can justify.

Returning to the earlier history, let us note that the king, being the foremost and indispensable champion of the Common Law in its infancy, was himself the greatest officer of state. Hence, when he used his authority to provide more adequate means for the administration of uniform justice, it was possible for lords of private jurisdictions, or other persons whose privileges were threatened, to represent his action in a sinister light as an encroachment of arbitrary discretion on ancient custom, thus reviving the prehistoric repugnance to allowing any judicial discretion at all. There is in truth all the difference in the world between increasing the resources of a procedure which is open to all men and assuming to withdraw particular cases from the scope of ordinary process, or interfering to dictate the result. But the popular instinct is not always instructed and hardly ever discriminates; and so monopolists may lead it by the nose under pretence of maintaining individual freedom. In the thirteenth century one of the Barons' grievances was the inventiveness of the king's clerks in his Chancery, who sought to extend the jurisdiction of the royal judges by framing new writs. By the Provisions of Oxford (A.D. 1257–58) an oath was imposed on the Chancellor that he would seal no writ that was not in common course except by the order of the king and his council. The later Statute of Westminster (A.D. 1275), which defined the scope of actions on the case, represents not a simple movement of expansion, but a compromise between advanced ideas and obstructive archaism. It must be allowed that the danger of arbitrary interference with the course of justice was by no means imaginary. As late as 1313 we find the king commanding justices in eyre to expedite a cause, with open avowal of personal interest in one of the parties, and (what is more) the justices turning a deaf ear to counsel's objection that the writ in the action is out of time under a statute regulating proceedings in the eyre, and therefore the court has no jurisdiction. The only answer counsel can get is that the judges cannot dispute the king's authority, and if it were necessary to presume a statute they would presume it. 'What the king commands we must suppose to be commanded by the General Council.'[1] It was natural enough for the king to suppose that he could do as he pleased in his own court although his judges could not; only fuller experience made it clear that the efficiency and the repute of the king's justice depended upon an inflexible understanding that no executive authority, not even the king's will, could meddle with its rules. In England we have now delegated large powers of regulation to the judges themselves. It is far from clear that it would have been safe to do so at any time before the Revolution. Interference with the ordinary process of the Court has, of course, nothing to do with the extraordinary or residuary power regularly attributed to the king, down to the seventeenth century, of doing justice in cases where for any reason the ordinary means were ineffective. The later orthodox doctrine, from any scientific point of view quite as arbitrary as the prerogative claims it displaced, was that this royal power or duty had exhausted itself in the establishment of the Court of Chancery, and that the jurisdiction of the Star Chamber, or rather of the king's Council in the Star Chamber, was lawful only so far as it was created or confirmed by statute. One thing is certain, however, which is of the first importance, and has been justly made prominent by all recent authors on the English constitution. No one ever maintained that the king's command, however express, would of itself justify or excuse an

---

[1] 'Qant le Roy maunde deit home supposer qe ceo soit per comune consail. Et dautre part home ne deit mye contrepleder le fait le Roy.' Eyre of Kent, 6 and 7 Ed. II, Selden Soc., 1910, pp. lxxxiii, 161, 176. The king's letter (p. 158) professes to desire expedition only 'selont la ley et lusage de nostre Roiaume et le cours del eire,' but admits that 'nous avoms ses bosoignes molt a cuer.'

act not warranted by the law of the land; much less that his officers could derive any protection from his general authority. The sheriff's responsibility to the king's subjects even for honest mistakes in the execution of his office is very ancient. It extends, and appears always to have extended, to acts of the sheriff's deputy or subordinate officers done without his personal knowledge. Perhaps it is our earliest example, outside the family or household, of the general rule summed up in the words 'respondeat superior.'

Next we have to consider the open enemies of law and legal order in modern times. We do not mean ordinary criminals, for lawbreakers, occasional or habitual, do not undertake at this day to subvert the law, but only do their best to thwart or evade it in their own particular interests. Again there is no need to dwell on those who speak evil of the legal profession rather than of the law itself. The common topics of vulgar abuse have been abundantly refuted by English authors, lay and professional, from Dr. Johnson to my lamented and accomplished friend Dr. Showell Rogers of Birmingham.[1]   Least of all is it needful to dwell on such matters in this country, where the canon of professional ethics has been so thoroughly discussed and .formulated. Enough to say that the rules accepted by American and English lawyers alike, whether in written form or unwritten, aim as high as those of any other calling in the world, and on the whole are·as well observed. Betrayal of a client's confidence is so rare as to be practically unheard of ; and in this point of honour the three learned faculties have long emulated one another on an equal footing of inflexible discipline. Laxity and even fraud in dealing with the

[1] The Ethics of Advocacy, L. Q. R. xv. 259.

property of clients are, unfortunately, by no means unknown, but I venture to think they are less common than in other kinds of business which offer like temptations. The only professional abuse, short of actual malversation, which is both facile and frequent is that of encouraging speculative and unsubstantial claims for the sake of making costs. Here it may be observed that the pursuit of hopeless causes is in fact oftener due to the client's obstinacy than to the lawyer's contrivance; nor does experience show that litigants, when they appear in person, are less litigious or more scrupulous than their advocates would have been for them. Nevertheless there is a real evil. It can be largely mitigated, under any simplified and rational scheme of procedure, by the firm application of judicial discretion. It could not be wholly prevented without investing the Court, from the very commencement of proceedings, with such inquisitorial functions as would make the remedy worse than the disease in the eyes of English-speaking people. Our lady the Common Law will mend her clothes and alter their fashion moderately from time to time; she will not take to garments of such incongruous cut that her friends would not know her in them.

As to complaints against the law in general, every man who loses a cause is apt to think that the law must be unjust or his counsellor incompetent; and since in every contentious cause at least one party must lose, it is obvious that complaint of this kind must abound. Much more subtle, and more dangerous because mixed with worthier motives than merely personal interest, is the dissatisfaction of such men as mislike the law when legal justice withstands the demands of their trade or their class. Law, being bound to regard the good of the commonwealth as a whole, must needs curb the partial ambition of both individuals and sections. Mistakes are possible, no doubt, in that process, as in all human endeavours to do justice. But it is not to be hastily assumed that bodies of men who demand advantages or immunities for themselves are likely to have as clear a sense of right as those whose business it is to be just to all. It is true that in controversies of this kind there may be real conflict of social and economic ideals, and that the doctrines prevailing in the Courts will almost inevitably be those of the older rather than the younger generation. But again there is no presumption either way that one or the other view is the sounder or contains more permanent elements of truth. There are such things as transitory dogmatic delusions, and novelties must overcome a certain amount of legitimate resistance if they are to prove their title to be taken into the common stock of a sane world. In a later discourse we shall return to these matters from a slightly different point·of view.

It is certain, in any case, that.far more class grievances have been raised by legislation than by the purely judicial development of the common law. From the Statute of Labourers downwards the legislature has constantly imposed on the Courts its own solution of the novel problems raised by social and economic changes. That solution, right or wrong, has always been dictated by the prevalent opinion among the governing classes and interests, in which lawyers, as such, have no more part than any other citizens. Not only legal experts cannot be made responsible for a large part of social legislation in substance, but their attempts to secure a tolerably workmanlike form for its expression have had very partial success, and sometimes have been wilfully disregarded by promoters who

care little for the faults of a showy enterprise if they can
score an advantage to their party by hurrying it through.
So far indeed are lawyers from having any particular love
for legislators that some of our classical authorities exhibit
a tendency to regard legislation as a natural enemy of the
law. Quite recently the late Mr. Carter of New York
(giving, I think, excessive reasons for mainly sound con-
clusions against an ill-informed and ill-framed project)
followed in the path of Sir Edward Coke. Most of us will
not go that length. It is too rash to affirm in general, and
without respect to differences of time, place, constitutional
methods, and other circumstances, that legislation is more
likely to be foolish than wise. On the other hand it would
be more than rash to affirm that, among the well meant
statutory reforms of our law, neither few nor unambitious,
any great proportion have achieved complete success in
reputation or in fact. Let us take, as a pretty familiar
subject, the great series of real property statutes from the
thirteenth century onwards, which for the most part are
as fully received here as in England. Only two of them,
I think, can be said to have met with general approval,
an early and a rather late one. The earlier is the statute
of Quia Emptores, which abolished subinfeudation — the
creation of new lordships and tenures intermediate between the ultimate lord and the actual freeholder [1] — and
may be said to have knocked the bottom out of feudalism
as a working theory of English law. We may note for
curiosity that William Penn's charter of 1681 contained,
among other ample and regal franchises, a dispensation
from Quia Emptores, by force whereof, as I understand,

[1] The words 'in fee simple' should be added if the statement is to be
strictly correct. But in practice the effect was unlimited.

E

in the State of Pennsylvania rents are reserved on conveyances in fee simple to this day;[1] likewise that our Scottish neighbours contrive to do their modern real estate business well enough with forms which are quite logically feudal. Still Quia Emptores was an excellent piece of work, anticipating indeed the methods of our best modern draftsmen, and no one in England ever wanted to amend it. The later example is the statute, commonly called of Wards and Liveries, which abolished military tenures and their incidents at the restoration of Charles II, in substance re-enacting the work of the Commonwealth. Its workmanship did not escape learned criticism, but the business was needful and was done once for all. Between these two great Acts we have in the thirteenth century the statute De Donis, purporting to make entails perpetual, which the lawyers protested against with all their might and helped their clients of the rising middle class to evade; and the Statute of Uses in the sixteenth century, so hastily and unskilfully framed that instead of simplifying tenure and conveyance it made them a worse tangle than before. These two most unhappy feats of legislative interference are answerable, to the best of my belief, and I think I may say in the general opinion of historical students of our law, for nearly the whole of the extraordinary complication in which dealings with land are still involved in England to a great and highly inconvenient extent, and in varying and more or less inconvenient degrees in other Common Law jurisdictions. I confess I do not know who framed the Statute of Uses, or whether the framers aimed at any result beyond securing the king's revenue; nor have I so

---

[1] As to the complication added to the Pennsylvanian doctrine, it seems without sufficient cause, by a modern decision, see Gray on Perpetuities, § 26.

much as heard whether any one has seriously tried to find out. It might be an interesting theme for some young scholar on this Continent or at the antipodes: for our generation has lived to welcome learned lawyers and keen historians from Australasia as well as from the Atlantic shores and from the heart of Canada. As for the later real property statutes that were enacted on broadly similar lines in England and America during the nineteenth century, one must say of the English ones at any rate that they can claim only a relative success, being either simplification of routine and common forms or makeshift amendments not going to the root of the matter. In the minority of cases where the work was entrusted to really skilled hands it was ingeniously and elegantly done within the limits assigned.[1]

Various modern theorists, political or economical, are hostile to particular legal institutions or their existing forms; and hence it is easy for their opponents, and sometimes profitable, to charge them with conspiring against the very existence of law. Concerning Socialism in its many forms, there is plenty of room for legitimate criticism, but antinomian heresy seems to be about the last kind that it can reasonably be accused of. For the one thing in which all socialist plans agree is in requiring not less legal compulsion than is imposed by existing civilized governments, but a great deal more, though the law to be enforced would in many respects be novel both in its actual contents and in the scale of social values it would lay down or assume. In any conceivable socialist legislation and jurisprudence public law, for one thing, would be magnified at the cost of private law, since individual discretion

---

[1] The Act for the abolition of Fines and Recoveries, framed by Mr. Brodie, is a classic of conveyancing draftsmanship.

would be supplanted by State regulation in many parts of the conduct of life where it is now tolerated or even encouraged. A strike would no longer be the exercise by divers citizens in combination of their individual right to work only on their own terms, but an act of rebellion against the public authority. We might like to be governed in that fashion or not, but it would be absurd to call a minutely regulated society lawless. Herein we may note that some persons who have been called or even have called themselves socialists were really anarchists; William Morris, for example, as shown by his 'News from Nowhere,' which, whatever else it be, is the most delightful exposition of pacific anarchism [1] in our language. That idyllic life in a regenerate England, as Morris conceives it, is life not under a paternal or fraternal executive, however democratically appointed, but without any executive at all; there is not a State which has appropriated capital and administers it for the common good, but the State has disappeared and capital has, apparently, been distributed among a number of very small autonomous communities whose members are wonderfully unanimous as to the use of it. Socialism properly so called presents the question (of no special import for us here) what kind of law would be fitted to carry out its economic ideals. Anarchism raises a much more curious problem, whether William Morris's or Tolstoy's Utopia would really succeed in getting rid of law so neatly or completely as the inventor thought. If the Morrisians or Tolstoyans could not agree, their only remedy would be to split up into smaller bodies each with

---

[1] We have nothing to say here of any other kind. The teaching of university schools is and ought to be comprehensive, but I know of no Faculty that has to teach the sheriff his business.

its own habits. The splitting process would however be limited, in the last resort, by the numbers of the smallest social unit capable of permanently supporting itself. Smaller or larger, the final units would be held together by something outside the wills of their individual members; and that something, being a force of habit which would be uniform, binding, and applicable to a definite independent group, would be very like what we know as customary law. Such a society might claim to justify its name of anarchist in so far as it knew nothing of a formal court or of those 'names of office' which Bentham considered the most decisive mark of established government. But one may doubt whether it could be wholly antinomian unless it relapsed into a state of internecine warfare between very small and unstable groups, which would be Hobbes's state of nature. No such catastrophe being contemplated by William Morris, Tolstoy, or to add a living name, Prince Kropotkin, its consequences do not enter into the consideration of their doctrine from the point of view of classification, or of ascertaining its essential contents. If, on the other hand, all the Utopians did agree, they would live under a custom that would be no less their rule of life because a blessed unanimity would make it needless for them so much as to think of enforcing it. And surely this is what William Morris did contemplate. One might go near to say that a commonwealth where no judge and no sheriff was wanted, and yet every man knew quite well what to expect of his fellow, would, so far from being lawless, exhibit the perfection of law. But the pursuit of the many puzzles ingeniously concealed by the charming artistic simplicity of 'News from Nowhere' would lead us too far, though on a proper occasion it might be a very pretty exercise.

It seems rather idle to ask whether the Common Law is individualist or socialist: it is both and neither. As against some socialist opinions, including perhaps those which are most in fashion just now, it has maintained the rights and the discretion of the individual, and maintained them strongly. Moreover, if I may borrow a phrase used a good many years ago by my learned friend Mr Phelps, the Common Law does its best to secure equality of legal rights, but disclaims any power to secure equality of conditions for all men. Our lady is a shrewd old lady, and has seen too many failures to be over-sanguine about any plan for putting the whole world straight. But as against some dogmas of extreme individualism, our law might with equal truth be called socialist. Thus it has never allowed unlimited freedom of contract even within the sphere of acts not punishable in criminal jurisdiction; and the hands of enterprising grantors were stayed as long ago as the thirteenth century, when, attributing a kind of magic efficacy to the form of the grant, they thought for a season that they could create at their pleasure new-fangled estates and confer greater powers of disposition than they had themselves. Thus, again, the Common Law has always regarded the constitution of the family as a matter appertaining to the discretion of the Commonwealth and not of the individual; agreeing herein, in principle, with socialism as against anarchism, though differing with modern socialist projects as to the possible or expedient amount of regulation. We may note in passing that among such projects we find, along with much novel compulsion, some relaxation and displacement of existing rules. In itself this is no more surprising than the fact that under the Torrens system of registration a vendor of land is no longer bound to prove his title by producing a chain of assurances or other evidence of continuous lawful possession by himself and his ancestors for the last sixty or forty years. It may go some way, however, towards accounting for the popular confusion of socialism with anarchism. The fact that socialists and anarchists can join in attacking the established economic order is in itself no more remarkable than any other coalition, against a common enemy for the time being, of parties or sections who have nothing but enemies in common. On the whole there is no doubt that movements of social and economic opinion are capable of modifying legal as well as other institutions; but if we attend to the actual course of affairs we shall find that any such operation is effected not by the negation of law but by controlling its forms and instruments. Indeed it is notorious that in political convulsions the legal part of an established order has often fared the best. When the French Revolution had swept away the rank and privileges of the nobles, the substance of the civil law remained in other respects much as it had been before. Napoleon's codes were based on the customs and ordinances of the monarchy; they were found quite well fitted to serve, with a moderate amount of editing and local amendment, for the Province of Quebec, where the Revolution had never passed.

An acuter kind of conflict may arise when obedience is refused to the secular magistrate in the name of a higher spiritual authority. Conscience, right or wrong, can be a very stubborn thing, and has been known to wear out the law in minor matters, as in the case of the Quakers. Not that the Common Law is very tolerant of conscientious pretenders to a special revelation; as witness the anecdote, apocryphal though it may be, concerning Chief Justice Holt and

a certain prophet. We speak here, however, of the more
serious case where the dissenting conscience appeals to an
external and visible authority having a law of its own.   Here
we have not the State on one side and the individual on the
other, but independent powers face to face, with the regular
incidents (mostly but not always short of physical combat)
of friendly or unfriendly relations, diplomatic discussion,
treaties, compromises, and so forth.   During the Middle
Ages our lady the Common Law was in frequent strife with
the more ancient and, at those times, more highly organized
empire of the Church and the Canon Law.   Now and then
the strife might be said to be for independence rather than
for any privilege or particular exclusive jurisdiction.   Boundary questions, however, must come up whenever two or more
jurisdictions exist at the same time and place and are capable
of overlapping; and their occurrence, though it may imperil
peace, does not involve in itself any state of normal hostility.
Far more deliberate, though much less known to posterity,
was the attack made on the Common Law in America not
by Popes or bishops but by Puritans.   The settlers of Massachusetts refused to admit any authority but that of their
own enactments, tempered by a general deference to 'God's
word,' meaning thereby the text of the Mosaic law: not the
system of the great medieval Rabbis, but the letter of the
Pentateuch interpreted after their own fashion.   Such was
the prevailing temper, down to the eighteenth century,
throughout the New England States, and the zeal of Massachusetts was equalled or even exceeded elsewhere (I do not,
of course, refer to the spurious 'Blue Laws' of Connecticut;
the genuine examples are sufficient).   Besides the constant
Puritanic or Judaizing bias, these early colonial ordinances
exhibit curious reversions to archaic ideas and classification.

Outside New England there was not the same downright aversion to English law and procedure, but it would be hard to find even in Virginia or the Carolinas, within the same period, any received presumption in favour of the Common Law being the groundwork of local jurisprudence.[1] It may seem a paradox, but it is a fact which research more and more tends to confirm, that it was none of the Pilgrim Fathers, but the Fathers of the Constitution, who, in the very act of repudiating allegiance to king and parliament, enthroned our lady the Common Law on the western shores of the Atlantic.

There seems to be no ground for affirming that the Common Law is especially attached to any one form of government, or is incompatible with any that makes substantial provision for civic liberty and the representation of the governed. Those fundamental conditions may be satisfied in many ways, perhaps in ways not yet found out. It might be hard to say how much of our lady's house has been rebuilt, but it is sure that the fashion of the furniture has been changed many times. Henry VIII, not to say Edward I, would never have believed a man who prophesied that his successors, after losing most of their direct power and sinking for a short time into political insignificance, would regain a high degree of consideration and no contemptible measure of influence as confidential but impartial advisers[2] of their own Ministers. Yet through all this the Common

[1] Reinsch, English Common Law in the Early American Colonies, in Select Essays in Anglo-American Legal Hist., i. 369, from whom I take the facts.

[2] It is not easy to find an unexceptionable word: the fact, partly revealed and partly guessed before, is now made plain by Queen Victoria's correspondence. I think it may be truly said that her counsels prevailed oftener than not, and not because she was the Queen, but because they were right and carried conviction.

Law stands where it did. Our lady does not, in truth, care much by what name the chief magistrate is called, whether his office is elective or hereditary, whether he has as much active discretion of his own as the President of the United States or as little as a modern King of Great Britain. What she does care for is that government, whatever its forms, shall be lawful and not arbitrary; that it shall have the essential attribute for which Chief Justice Fortescue's word was 'political' as far back as the fifteenth century. She looks for trusty servants who will stand by her in the day of need. She demands fearless and independent judges drawn from a fearless and independent Bar, men who will not swerve from the straight path to the right hand for any pleasure of rulers, be they aristocratic or democratic, nor be drawn aside to the left by the more insidious temptation of finding popular favour in opposition. If our lady's servants are not of that spirit, all the learning of all their books will not save them from disgrace or her realm from ruin. If they are, we shall never see the enemy whom she and they will be afraid to speak with in the gate.

V. RESCUE AND RANSOM

HAVING now seen something of the troubles that beset our lady and her servants at sundry stages of their pilgrimage, we may well be curious about the remedies: and here we must deal tenderly with lay common sense, which may be apt to think that we are making a great fuss and mystery about nothing to magnify the importance of our Faculty. The plain man is ready enough to believe that the Common Law has had outworn and cumbrous tools to work with. What he does not so readily see is why we should not scrap our old plant like other modern men of business, and say no more about it; or for that matter why it was not done centuries ago. — So simple a thing, he will say, for you lawyers to devise new and better forms; you have not even cost of materials to reckon with; nothing but pen and ink — yes, and brains, I know; but without brains no business of any kind gets done. Did King Henry II sit up o' nights over the Assize of Novel Disseisin, whatever that may have been? Well, I suppose that was what he was king for. — My dear man, answers our lady the Common Law, I have to tell you that it was just you lay people, as often as not, who hindered my servants from improving things in the simplest way when they were eager to do it, and drove them into making their improvements by crooked devices, to the great disparagement of my honour and worship, and useless charges and vexation of my suitors. — Will the worthy layman believe that? Our time is full short to convince him if he does not

59

already know the facts. We can only give him a few of them in the time we have.

One fact is that in the thirteenth century the king's judges and clerks were ready to provide new forms of writs to meet the growing demand for the king's justice. That was the rational and straightforward course. It was no fault of theirs that their beneficent invention was checked by jealousy, the jealousy not of any professional vested interest but of outside interests and privileges. Many great lords, many smaller ones too, had their private jurisdictions or judicial franchises [1] and derived much profit from them in fees and fines. If the king's justice had a free hand, their privilege and profit would be assailed by novel and irresistible methods of competition. I cannot affirm that their jealousy was reinforced by the ancient popular distrust of official experts and the superstitious popular sentiment which, except under pressure of an immediate grievance, looks on innovation of any kind with fear and dislike; but I cannot think it improbable. In any case the skilled reformers were not allowed to carry out their intention. The profession and the suitors were put off with the half-hearted recognition of Actions on the Case, which amounted, in untechnical language, to saying that new remedies might not be introduced except under pretense of being variations on old ones. Whether the lords of private courts were any the better for this may be doubted. They did not know that our lady the Common Law was to have much of King Edward I's heart in her governance, and had Quo Warranto up her sleeve for him that therewith he might teach arrogant lords their place. But that story is not for us here. Again, skipping some cen-

---

[1] The profits of justice which was originally public or royal could be appropriated in various ways, and not seldom were.

turies, we may ask the judicious critic to note that no less a publicist than Junius denounced Lord Mansfield's reforms, universally approved by later generations, as arbitrary corruptions of the law and encroachments on the liberties of Englishmen, substituting his own unsettled notions of equity for positive rules.   In one sense, indeed, it is true enough that you can hardly expect reform if you are not prepared to interfere with liberties: namely if you take the word 'liberty' in the sense it regularly bears in medieval Latin, which is a right, by way of monopoly, custom or otherwise as it may be, to get all you can out of somebody.   This may seem less paradoxical when we remember that 'franchise' is only the French equivalent of *libertas*.

Intelligent laymen, to be sure, have tried their hand at contributing to law reform, but they have not been invariably successful even in our enlightened age.   A certain well meant amateur addition to one of our English Companies Acts was fruitful of litigation and costs until, a few years ago, it perished unlamented in the general revision of a consolidating Act.   Another recent example is perhaps more instructive.   In the latter years of the nineteenth century, notwithstanding the reconstruction of our judicial system in 1875 and the merger of all special jurisdictions in the universal powers of the High Court, there was much complaint among London business men of delay in hearing commercial causes in the Queen's Bench Division.   An elaborate scheme for a voluntary tribunal of arbitration was framed by a combination of legal and mercantile wits, and the names of many distinguished lawyers were placed on the rota of arbitrators. It was a mighty pretty scheme, but its promise was cut short in an unexpected manner.   Lord Gorell (then Justice Gorell Barnes of the Probate and Admiralty Division) gave

out one day[1] that he was ready to put causes of a commercial
kind in a special list, expedite all interlocutory stages, and
abridge or wholly dispense with pleadings, if the parties
would only undertake not to raise merely technical points
and to admit all substantially uncontested facts. He also
gave a hint that (the actual jurisdiction being undoubted
under the Judicature Act) it would not be the Court that
would ask whether any particular cause were exactly an
Admiralty matter. This pioneer experiment was speedily
followed by the common-law judges,[2] who established the
so-called Commercial Court by a simple exercise of administrative discretion.[3] It is in truth not a distinct court, but
a special cause list open to parties on the understanding
devised in the first instance by Justice Gorell Barnes, and
assigned to a judge familiar with commercial matters. The
arrangement works excellently, and nothing more is heard
of the grand arbitration scheme which was to relieve the
congested courts and display the superior resources of private
enterprise.[4] Of all this the general public knows nothing
and some lawyers very little; for it was done with no controversy and an absolute minimum of formality. Sure I
am that for so complete and peaceful a triumph of rational
procedure Lord Gorell and his companions have earned our
lady's most benignant smile. It remains true that lawyers
tend, for the more part, to cling to the tradition, good or bad,
ancient or recent, in which they were trained. But when
reforms have been carried against the majority of the pro-

[1] In 1893 · see L. Q. R. ix. 373.

[2] This, though no longer officially correct since 1875, is still a current and
convenient term in the profession.

[3] In 1895, see Encycl. Laws of England, s.v. 'Commercial Court.'

[4] We shall not forget that there was and is a great deal of private and quite
informal arbitration, nor think it any reproach to the law that this, whenever
practicable, is a better way than litigation.

fession, I think it has always been by the exertions of a keen and able professional minority who cared much more about their cause than the public whom they persuaded to support them.

These preliminary remarks make no claim to be exhaustive or systematic. It is enough to have shown that correction of the evils due to formalism and stagnation is not such an easy matter as it looks, and that the blame of failure, when it occurs, is not always due to the lawyers. We will now try to classify the remedial methods: they are all more or less artificial, and sometimes they involve an element of pious fraud, or rather (for it has a better sound in Latin) *dolus bonus*. The most ancient way is to call in aid authorities and jurisdictions which in their origin were extraordinary, and which just for that reason still have some discretionary freedom. The next is to extend and develop the more convenient modes of procedure at the expense of the less convenient; and here we find the uses of fiction, that sadly misunderstood instrument of justice. The third method, effective if employed with due skill and knowledge, is the specific amendment of what is amiss by some form of legislative authority. A fourth and very modern way is the systematic reconstruction of procedure as a whole, a dispensation under which many of us are now living. In this, as likewise in partial improvement by legislation, the power employed may be either direct or delegated.

First, then, the use of extraordinary jurisdiction to circumvent the defects of ordinary forms is the royal road in every sense for so long as it is practicable. By that method the superior courts, as we knew them from the thirteenth to the nineteenth century, were established. The doctrine of the twelfth century under Henry II, is that the hundred and county courts are still the instruments of ordinary justice. There is a list of criminal matters reserved for the king, as a certain number were even before the Norman Conquest: in civil matters the king as overlord has original jurisdiction over his own immediate tenants, and to a considerable extent he can supersede the county court in other cases. A great mass of minor business is left to the popular courts, or to the seignorial and other special jurisdictions which are actively competing with them. Still the king's justice is fast growing in importance, and it is thought proper that an officer of its inner circle should write a manual of its practice under the Justiciar's patronage. About a century later we find that the king's court has definitely come to the front, and a body of learned persons permanently attached to it as judges, clerks and practitioners is already formed. There are still pretty large gaps in the jurisdiction, but the judges are eager to fill them. If their efforts are not wholly successful, it is not from the profession, as we have already noticed, that the difficulties come. In one region, indeed, that of contract, law and procedure are rudimentary, and have to remain so for about two centuries more. Here however we must remember that the materials, in the actual state of business among Englishmen, are rudimentary likewise, outside the sphere of the law merchant, and external trade is for the most part in the hands of foreigners who settle their affairs within their own gilds or in the market courts. The hundred court is moribund and the county court is kept alive in strict subordination to the king's judges, it would seem chiefly for the purpose of collecting the king's fines. But there is already a less favourable side to the picture. One cannot have an elaborate and far-reaching official system for nothing. In becoming highly organized

the king's justice has become formalized, though not after
the archaic fashion. No room is left for patriarchal inter-
vention like the Conqueror's or even Henry II's. Forms
of action are inflexible, precedents are binding, judges know
and counsel are ready to remind them, that the judgments
they make on any new question will be law for their companions and successors. Moreover the complaints of great
men defying the law have not ceased. The hands of the
king's judges are valiant in his work, but there is much left
that only the king in his Council can do. Learned canonists
and civilians are not wanting who boast of their summary
procedure; and it is like enough that in some dioceses and
archdeaconries people who are in the ale-house when they
ought to be in church, or perjure themselves, or commit
other scandalous actions, do find the process of the Court
Christian more summary than they desire.

Accordingly we have no cause for surprise when, after
another century, we see the Chancellor's jurisdiction rising
and becoming popular. We may learn from Blackstone,
who followed his Elizabethan authorities quite correctly, that
it was founded in the king's unexhausted duty to see justice
done where the ordinary means fell short or were frustrated.
Equitable jurisdiction, coming so late on the scene, had to
go through a stage of conflict with the older courts at Westminster, and long remained a thing apart from the Common
Law in the most specific sense of that term. It so remains
in some jurisdictions even now. We may doubt whether
the conflict that took place in the days of Elizabeth and
James I was at all reasonably necessary; we may be sure
that it was aggravated by Coke's pseudo-antiquarian pedantry and the personal hostility between him and Bacon.
But at this day we can see that the growth of the Chan-

F

cellor's equity, and the fixing of it in a model as regular as
that of the common law (on which Blackstone again speaks
profitably), were really a continuation of the very same his-
toric process which began with Henry II's reforms and was
witnessed and confirmed by the Great Charter.   The development of auxiliary criminal jurisdiction in the Star Chamber
was exactly parallel (as Bacon has told us) and did quite
honest service for a century or more.   It was ruined not by
inherent vice but by abuse; the Star Chamber was doomed
when Charles I made it an engine of political and ecclesiastical persecution.   With it fell the whole method of in-
voking extraordinary jurisdiction to create new forms of
justice which in due course become ordinary.   Cut short by
violent death before our Civil War had begun, it must be
pronounced extinct on this earth.   We cannot tell whether
long life or honourable euthanasia would have been its portion
if the Stuart kings had been masters of a different kind of
statecraft from that which they exhibited in fact.   There
may or may not be some innocent reason in the judicial
nature of things why the art of drawing as required on the
king's reserved treasures of justice must in any case have
lost its virtue.   I see no such reason myself.   It rather
pleases me to dream of some planet where a dynasty of wise
rulers, escaping religious distractions and civil strife, established responsible government at a stage (let us say)
corresponding to our politically barren fifteenth century;
where judicial discretion doing its best to be impartial is not
hampered at every turn by the meddling of partisan statutes
with their crude remedies of contrary excess, first one way
and then the other, for the grievances of successive generations; where nobody pretends to be infallible, and not honest
mistake is censured, but obstinate refusal to acknowledge

and repair it; where Orders in Council, carefully framed by the servants of the State with the best skill available and after all due consultation, and operative by an inherent authority which it has never been necessary to dispute, provide for most administrative needs; where commissions of inquiry are a serious and judicial preparation for action; where matters of principle are gravely and fruitfully discussed in an assembly whose considered opinion is the policy of the realm; and where formal legislation, other than for financial purposes, is rather an exceptional solemnity. I do not ask whether a party system either of the British or of the American type deserves a place in that dream; it is not a question of law, therefore not fit to be considered here.

Secondly, there is some consolation in extending old jurisdictions, if you cannot make new ones. Here our lady the Common Law smiles a little at those who wonder that she favours economic competition and dislikes monopoly. 'How should I not approve competition,' she whispers to her more discreet apprentices, 'when I owe so much of my resources to the competition of my servants for fees? All through the Middle Ages and even later jurisdiction meant fees and profits; or do you really think thirteenth-century lords (including bishops and mayors) took a sentimental pride in hanging their own thieves? My sister Canonica may purse up her mouth if she likes, as who should say that in her kingdom they know nothing of such vulgar motives. I am not denying her genuine zeal for the welfare of souls, and we all know that breach of faith is a sin. Still, would bishops and archdeacons have entertained suits in the Court Christian about a load of hay or a loan of pots and pans if there had been no profit in it? And if my servants had not found that between the king's Chancellor and the bishop's chancellors they were in danger of losing much good business, how much longer might I have waited for a rational doctrine of contract? Sister Canonica puts on her most precise air and all but sniffs; I know she will not believe we have made it rational yet. Well, I profess to hold people to their bargains, and not to hold them to promises that are not bargains unless they choose to make it a solemn affair. After all, is not that common sense? My sister holds out in one hand the profession of enforcing all serious promises, and takes away most of it with the other by means of artificial exceptions and rules of proof. I like my own way better. As for having reached a tolerably simple conclusion by devious and puzzling ways, we have both done too much of that to criticize one another.' But we must respect our lady's confidences; perhaps we have already gone to the verge of prudence.

Just now that which directly interests us is not so much the competition for business between rival courts as the competition within our own house between different methods of procedure, old and new, permanent and experimental, of which the most convenient or at any rate the least inconvenient came out successful. At the same time this operation was an indispensable factor in actual extensions of the jurisdiction. The tool which had to be handled for all or almost all the work was the action on the case; and we shall find it curious to remark on how narrow a foundation the great superstructure of our classical common law was built. In a general way there was nothing to prevent an action analogous to any of the settled forms being framed 'in a like case.' But in fact the more ancient forms were too stubborn to be dealt with in this manner; not by reason of anything in the cause of action itself, but because they were entangled in cumbrous and awkward points of procedure at every stage. Here we may learn something from the little noticed mistake of a great author. Blackstone conjectured that the action of Assumpsit, the regular modern action of contract, was the action on the case answering to the thirteenth-century writ of Covenant: a clever but rash and baseless conjecture, and hardly excusable, for without going farther back than Coke's Reports he might have known that it was originally founded in tort. Now in fact there was nothing to be done in that way with Debt or Covenant, or even with Account, which at first sight might look more tractable. The only forms that would really serve were those of the later thirteenth century which had a specially royal and official character, and therefore were fairly free from archaic incidents, namely Trespass and Deceit. All our modern remedies in the Common Law, so far as concerns ordinary civil affairs, are the offspring of one or the other; Assumpsit, by a peculiar combination, of both. Trespass protected and still protects actual possession; its analogous extensions protect the right to possess, as distinct (not necessarily separated) from possession itself, in corporeal things, and also the many categories of exclusive right in incorporeal things. We are not to conceive this process as exhausted in the Middle Ages or at any assignable time; it would be rash, in my opinion erroneous, to say that it is exhausted now. Not till after the Restoration was pleading on ordinary contracts and quasi-contracts immensely simplified by the bold and beneficent invention of the 'common counts' for goods sold and delivered, money paid, and so forth. Fraud not involving a breach of contract was long regarded as a matter that only the Court of Chancery could deal with, until in the latter part of the eighteenth century the common law jurisdiction attacked it with the action on the case for deceit. Later still, not much more than half a century ago, came the action for procuring breach of contract, allowed against learned and weighty dissent, continued in the face of more dissent and severe criticism, in jeopardy, as it seemed, within quite recent memory, and finally confirmed in England, and set on its true footing, only by judgments in the House of Lords and the Court of Appeal so recent that they passed through my hands as editor of the Law Reports. American jurisprudence, to its credit, was more firmly progressive on this delicate point. In our most modern stage, be it noted. opposition comes not from without but from within. Our lady the Common Law has many stout men doing her knight service, and some of them are more adventurous than others. Her landmarks have not been advanced without hesitation and partial retreats. In some cases imprudent expeditions, or indeed unlawful raids on the freedom of lawful men, have been properly restrained. On the other hand there have been regrettable checks, and for us in England some irreparable ones. My learned friend Professor Williston of Harvard is not too late in this country to lift up his voice against the narrow and inelegant decision of the House of Lords in *Derry* v. *Peek*. But it is becoming an old story, and I said long ago what I could say about that misfortune, as we of the Equity Bar thought it.

If the action on the case was the right hand of our lady's servants in extending her realm, the left hand was Fiction; or rather we should have to symbolize her as a Hindu goddess with many hands both right and left. By fiction the cumbrous real actions were all but laid on the shelf, and those two good stage carpenters John Doe and Richard Roe set a scene which they left clear for the speaking actors to play their parts without further hindrance.[1] By fiction, the fiction of conclusively presuming that a man had promised to pay what he owed, Assumpsit annexed the territory which formalism would have reserved for Debt. By a new and most ingenious fiction, almost in our own time, Willes and his brethren gave us a complete remedy for the case of an agent who professes, whether in good or in bad faith, to have an authority which he has not. True it is that the fiction was called for only by reason of a stupid maxim due to some unknown medieval bungler who had dabbled in Romanist phrases. By fiction our lady the Common Law borrowed the name of a still more exalted lady, St. Mary-le-Bow in the ward of Cheap, to stretch the power of her arm beyond the four seas, as Governor Mostyn learnt to his cost. It is easy to laugh at these and other fictions that our fathers made in their need. Their outer garb may be quaint, even grotesque; but in every case there was a sound principle of justice under these trappings, and the ends of justice could not be otherwise attained. Many were the suitors who invoked the aid of the king's Exchequer against persons alleged to be in their debt, and by default in payment to hinder them from paying their own dues to the king. No penny of those imaginary dues went into the royal accounts, but the writ of *Quo minus* turned the Exchequer from a mere revenue department into a court co-ordinate with the King's Bench and Common Pleas, and at last fully equal to them in strength and reputation. The King's Bench itself was not above laying hands on the pleas of subjects by a fiction even more

---

[1] It might have been better to simplify and rationalize the principal real actions, as indeed several American States have done. But it would take us altogether too far, in our present short course, to stop for discussion of what might have been; and let this apology cover other like cases as they occur.

transparent. Uniformity of Process Act, Common Law Procedure Acts, Judicature Acts, these in our fathers' time and our own took down the queer untidy scaffolding of procedural devices; but without the scaffolding the builders could not have worked.

The third remedial method is the most obvious and at first sight should be the most useful, namely, specific amendment by legislation directed to particular defects as they are discovered or come to be more urgently felt. Without doubt this is a serviceable instrument when rightly handled, but in unskilful hands it can be a remedy worse than the disease. Until our own time it was commonly treated as belonging to the technical part of the law, and left to the leaders of the profession. It is much older than we commonly recognize. Much of the familiar everyday process in our courts of law rests on medieval statutes which not one modern lawyer in a hundred has ever looked at; all power to deal with costs, for example, is derived from statutes. The partial reforms in pleading effected in the early part of the eighteenth century and commemorated, as we have already seen, by Blackstone, are almost as little remembered at this day. Many provisions of this kind have become obsolete and are superseded by better or more comprehensive enactments. It is probable that some were never anything but mistakes, for good lawyers may fall into bad mistakes of policy. Some, it is certain, were mere failures, proving inoperative in practice from one or another unforeseen cause. At best there are points of inherent weakness in these occasional repairs. Even a tinker of genius cannot get beyond tinkering, and tinkers are not men of genius as a rule. There is no security for any uniform plan being followed, or even for the workman of to-day having any clear understanding of what those before him have done. Indeed, it is often hard enough for experts, after a long course of statutory patching and mending, to know what the result amounts to, and how much of it was intended. Then the modern conditions of legislative discussion have brought in the danger of amateur meddling, and the not very desirable antidote of purposely framing technical amendments in the form least intelligible and most repulsive to the lay mind. Much has been said in reproach of lawyers, but there is more and worse to be said, if we chose to say it, against the man of business who thinks he knows better. The foregoing remarks are also more or less applicable to the mechanism of larger constructive changes in the substance of the law, which however is not immediately before us. On the whole, the genius of the Common Law works here in a turbid medium where 'the gladsome light of jurisprudence' is apt to be sadly obscured. This is in some measure the fault of the profession itself. Both judges and practitioners have often lacked either the wit to know or the will to try how much could be done without legislation.

The fourth and latest way of amendment we have to note is deliberate reconstruction of jurisdiction and procedure on a large scale: a heroic method adopted in many countries outside the Common Law, but oftener than not for political or national rather than purely legal reasons. One may find it associated, as in the codes of continental Europe, with systematic recasting of the substantive law itself, but this has not been the usual way of the Common Law. One great drawback to extensive schemes of this kind has been the neglect to make any regular provision for future amendment; hence arises danger of the new model becoming stereotyped and begetting new formalism of its own, which in time may be little better than the old. Periodical revision at fixed intervals has been often recommended but, so far as I know, seldom practised. In England we have found another way, less ambitious but not less effectual, by delegating a continuous regulating power to the Court. It is easier for our judges to supplement or amend the Rules of the Supreme Court (which are in substance a procedure code) than for the Government of India to revise its Procedure Codes even without the complication of the parliamentary machine and with the aid of an expert but overworked Legislative Department. In English-speaking countries all these things would be better done if professional zeal, when it is awakened, were backed by an intelligent public opinion. But we have allowed our art and mystery[1] to become a mystery, in the sense of the like-sounding and now more familiar word, to the lay people; and in this and other ways we have to pay for it. The best of all would be, once more, that the Courts should never be wanting in the knowledge of their own inherent powers and the courage to use them. But this achievement is of a felicity not reducible to classification or rule.

[1] *Ministerium* (mod. French *métier*) not *mysterium*.

VI. ALLIANCE AND CONQUEST

THUS far we have spoken of the Common Law militant, striving with troubles at home and opposed to hostile powers without. It is now time to speak of our lady's triumphs in enlarging her borders. Little or almost none of this was done by force, much by judicious alliance and voluntary commendation. She did not go forth in manner of war to make her conquests, but was rather like a wise prince whose neighbours gladly seek his friendship, whose policy binds them to him by the commerce of mutual benefits, and whose government is a profitable example. We may read in many books of what the Common Law has borrowed or is supposed to have borrowed from other systems. It was once fashionable to exaggerate the importance of these foreign elements; later, and within recent memory, there was risk of undue depreciation at the hands of a school dominated by the Germanic tendency which was part of the general nationalist revival in Europe in the nineteenth century. We must not enter here on these larger aspects of historical thinking; but we note for our own purposes that students of the Common Law, being lawyers but no historians, were too long at the mercy of historians and antiquaries who were no lawyers or, what is worse, indifferent amateurs in law. Through successive generations, for about two centuries, English text-writers were ready, now to ascribe magical influence to 'the civil law,' of which they seldom knew a word at first hand, now to swallow legends of a feudal system that never existed in England, or again to fly to the other extreme and swear by a 'mark system' that never existed anywhere. Rigorous in vouching and expecting authority for the assertion of any doctrine in their own law, they thought any kind of remote hearsay and unverified opinion good enough for historical fact. The prevalence of this uncritical temper may well be due to the bad example set by a great working lawyer whose mind was thoroughly unhistorical, Sir Edward Coke.[1] If Coke had been endowed with the scholarly method of a Spelman (to set up a mark more within reach than John Selden's unique learning and judgment) we might perhaps have had a historical school before the Germans. At this day we know that firm ground can be attained only by a training both legal and historical: the best of our law schools have already worked on this line long enough to show much good fruit and the promise of more. Let us now come to the facts; we must be content to deal with such as are well established, and I think we shall find those, taking them broadly as they stand, sufficient.

The Common Law, like the English language,[2] contains a great deal of mixed and composite material, but has an individual structure and character which are all its own; and,

[1] One or two recent writers have gone the length of calling Coke illiterate but this is an unjust reproach. His Latin prefaces are not classical, but they do not pretend to be, and there is nothing to show that he had any trouble in writing them. He was not a scholar like Bacon, very few lawyers were.

[2] It must not be supposed that English is alone in this respect. Modern Persian offers a remarkable analogy both in its wealth of adopted Arabic words and in its extreme grammatical simplicity. My Oriental studies are too slight to enable me to say how much attention this analogy has received from philologists. In Urdú, the current polite language of Northern India, we have a large Persian vocabulary, including much imported Arabic, added to a Hindí stock of which the original structure is unchanged. In both cases there has been large adoption of exotic literary form; there does not seem, however, to be any parallel in either to the organic influence which the Romance elements have exercised in English.

also like the English language, has on the whole had the best of it in competition with rivals. There is no case, I believe, of the Common Law having lost ground in presence of another system; there are certainly many where it has gained, and the question is forced on an inquiring mind, to use the words of a recent ingenious French writer: "A quoi tient la supériorité des Anglo-Saxons?" Whatever we might say if we could throw ourselves back into Coke's frame of mind, we can surely not be content to say that it is due to the intrinsic virtues of our race, or altogether to the superior justice or convenience of our rules. The more we look into other civilized modern laws, the more we shall find that under all differences of terminology and procedure the results come out not much unlike. No sane and impartial man will believe that in the main there is not as good justice in Edinburgh as in London, or at Montreal as at Toronto. Besides, one thing the boldest champion could never say in our praise is that we take any pains to make our ways easy for strangers who have a mind to learn them. The fact remains that the Common Law shows an assimilative power which, to all appearance, grows by what it feeds on. Therefore it must have started, even in its rude infancy, with some definite advantage. The suggestion I am about to put forward does not purport to give a complete explanation, but I hope it is sound as far as it goes.

As it emerges into distinct view in the late twelfth and early thirteenth century, our law is perceived as wielding one jurisdiction among many; so far eminent, no doubt, as it is in a special manner the king's. But the king recognizes and protects the other jurisdictions too, if indeed, as regards the Church, there is any talk of protection rather than of equality or even claims to supremacy. Is there, then, any other distinctive character? Yes, there is this great difference, that other laws are special and personal, while the Common Law is not. It is the law not of a class or of a kindred, but of the whole kingdom and the men who dwell therein; *lex et consuetudo Angliæ* is its proper style. On the other hand the canon law, to take the case of the greatest rival, is personal though it is universal. Doubtless it is binding on all Christian men, but it is the law of Christians only; we do not speak here of the justice which many prelates, from the Pope downwards — say, for a domestic example, the Bishop of Durham — administer as temporal princes with territorial jurisdiction, for, though such justice may be bound in principle[1] to accord with the law of Holy Church, it is in itself not spiritual but secular. Doubtless, also, the Common Law assumes that the king's subjects in general are Christians in the obedience of the Church; it is by no means clear that others, Jews for example (if indeed this be not the only practical case) had any right to our lady's protection down to the end of the Middle Ages and even later[2]; but it is clear that all men dwelling on English ground have to abide English law, the law of the king's courts, unless they can show some special reason to the contrary. That, indeed, is what 'the common law' means. Therefore our lady the Common Law takes, as matter of course, whatever other jurisdictions

[1] In England the Bishop of Durham's secular law followed the king's so closely that his temporal court issued in his name prohibitions directed to himself as judge of his spiritual court.

[2] No one appears to have doubted Edward I's right to banish the Jews by a mere act of royal authority. Prynne, under the Commonwealth, wrote a violent controversial tract against their readmission, accepting all the medieval fables about sacrificial murder or circumcision of Christian children. Presumably the king might at any time have given his protection to individual Jews as an exceptional favour. But I rather think that, so far as the presence of Jews was winked at after the expulsion, the toleration was informal and precarious; nor was there ever any formal restitution.

have left for whatever reason, and keeps it with very little chance of losing it again. Moreover, being of a free hand, she knows how to take as well as to give nobly and without false shame, which is a high point of generosity and something of a divine secret. Her cloak will open as wide as the Madonna's, and the children she welcomes under it are adopted for her very own. Where the occasion was not ripe for full intimacy, she has been politic in making friends of rivals and possible adversaries.

Chief among her allies and companions is Equity, who has at last come to keep house with her in England though not in all her dominions. Their days of strife are over; it is not easy to be sure how much of the strife was genuine. On certain points there was definite conflict; but the sixteenth-century complaints which reiterate a general charge of administering vague and capricious natural justice may be thought to savour of controversial common form, employed to cover the unavowable motive of dislike to effectual competition. Anyhow, the battle of judgments and injunctions in which King James I and Bacon finally had their will of Coke seems to us nowadays a battle fought very long ago. There were other and later jealousies which crossed the Atlantic with the Puritans and have left pretty recent traces, if I mistake not, in some American jurisdictions; but the causes of these were more political than legal. At home the relations of law and equity, once put on a correct footing, became harmonious and profitable, and have steadily improved for more than two centuries. Each system, being compelled to understand something of the other, learnt also to know itself better. Equity has enriched the common law, the common law has clarified equity. We have discovered, of late years, at any rate, that many doctrines which had been supposed to be mysteries of the Chancery were in truth very good common law. We have done with the punctilio which forbade equity judges to decide a purely legal question; we have long known that a good equity lawyer must build on a solid common law foundation; real property law, indeed, may be said to have been too much left to specialists of the Chancery Bar in modern times. We have all but done with the old attitude of distant and formal respect veiling something like a contemptuous incredulity. Very soon it will cease to be possible for a man to have a reputation for skill in the Common Law without at least an elementary knowledge of equity. Readers of English reports of the last generation, in the early days of the so-called fusion, may, by this time, find a quaint archaic flavour in the confessions of ignorance uttered with a certain ostentation by sturdy common law judges of the old school. But, while Bramwell declared that he could attach no meaning to constructive fraud (having satisfied himself, presumably, that the constructive possession and constructive delivery of modern commercial law were simpler notions), Bowen could, with the utmost courtesy, and more justly and profitably, point out that Jessel, surpassed by none among recent equity lawyers, and perhaps equaled only by Cairns, had underrated the resources of the Common Law. With regard to the contributions made by equity jurisprudence to what is now the common stock, it is well known that they account for most of our Romanist importation. Here it is needful to call to mind the warning given a good many years ago by Langdell. The learning and procedure of the early Chancellors might well enough be called Roman, but not in the classical sense of modern scholars. As between the two rival branches of jurisprudence outside England, they belonged not to the civilian, but to the canonical side; and therefore, when we think we are on the track of Roman influence anywhere between the thirteenth and the seventeenth centuries, it is quite unscientific to jump to a modern edition of the Corpus Juris.

Some trafficking with canon law, but not much, came in a more direct way through contact with ecclesiastical jurisdiction; and maybe some with pure civilian learning, but very little from admiralty law. |The practitioners in those branches were quite separate in England from those of the Common Law till 1857, and indeed the law and procedure of our Probate Divorce and Admiralty Division retain most of their old special features to this day. Much more important were the relations of the Common Law with the cosmopolitan doctrine of the Law of Nature, certainly not the least notable product of medieval intellect.[1] Our grand pervading principle of Reasonableness, which may almost be called the life of the modern Common Law, is intimately connected with it. St. German, the first of our comparative jurists, pointed this out with admirable clearness in the forefront of his 'Doctor and Student,' but for about three centuries and a half he spoke to deaf ears. I have written of this matter elsewhere, and my friend and successor at Oxford, Professor Vinogradoff, worked out some details of great interest at the last Historical Congress in Berlin. During the classical period of medieval English law the king's judges were quite aware of the Law of Nature, and sometimes (though, as St. German says, not usually) appealed to it by name. This is a topic on which proper critical study of the later Year Books may yet bring us new light. We are however fairly well informed as

---

[1] Opinions may differ on the amount of originality shown by the lawyers and schoolmen of the Middle Ages in adapting their Greek and Latin material. My own estimate of it is very high.

G

to the most practical applied branch of the Law of Nature, namely, the Law Merchant. Here we find the greatest of our lady's acquisitions, the more remarkable because it was made in a generation not otherwise distinguished for creative power or large enterprise. The king's law had always recognized the law merchant as having its proper sphere; royal charters even prescribed its use.[1] There were sporadic attempts at pleading it in ordinary litigation, first avowedly, later by fictions of special local custom. But it clearly would not do for the king's courts to admit parties to be judged by any other law than the king's, and in the absence of a general doctrine of contract there was no other way. When the action of Assumpsit had enlarged not only procedure but ideas, mercantile causes could be brought before the court on the footing, not that the parties were persons subject to the law merchant, but that they had agreed to be bound by the custom of merchants. In this sense it could be said in the seventeenth century that the law merchant was part of the Common Law: Blackstone had no difficulty in adopting this statement, writing just before Lord Mansfield's work began. We do not know exactly why business men wanted, after the Restoration, to come into the king's court, but we may surmise that on the one hand the domestic jurisdiction of trade gilds, whether of Englishmen or of foreigners in England, had broken down for economic reasons, and, on the other hand, the summary process of local market and maritime courts failed to insure much certainty in the substance of their judgments. Perhaps, too, the executive powers of the local courts, in spite of their customs of attachment, left something to be desired. In London the aid of the Chancellor

[1] As in the Court of Yarmouth Fair, *temp.* Ed. I.   Montagu Burrows, Cinque Ports, 170.

had been invoked to determine the commercial matters of strangers by 'the law of nature in the Chancery'; the practice was to refer the case to a commission of merchants, and Malynes, who tells us this, also tells us that [it was not expeditious. Only two steps more were needed to complete the desired transfer to common law jurisdiction. The first was to treat the averment of the parties having contracted according to the custom of merchants as merely formal, or the form of the instrument itself as conclusive evidence of that intention; and this was done in the early part of the eighteenth century at latest. The second, which was reserved for Lord Mansfield, was that the Court should not treat the law merchant as an exotic law to be proved by evidence in every case, but should be bold to take judicial notice in the future of what had once come to its knowledge. Thus general mercantile custom, provided it were really general, became in the fullest sense matter of law. From the point of view of the Common Law the triumph was perfect. The Law Merchant, however, had to pay her footing for admission to our lady's house by submitting to the procedure of the common law courts and its incidents, including legislative regulation such as the Statute of Frauds. In the middle of the nineteenth century Parliament made amends by providing a new summary procedure on bills of exchange, afterwards extended to all liquidated demands to which it appears, on the proper interlocutory application, that there is no substantial defense. Remembering that in England, at any rate, the majority of actions are undefended, we cannot doubt that Order XIV (so it stands in our Rules of the Supreme Court) is among the most beneficent inventions of modern procedure; and the history shows that indirectly we owe it to the law merchant. For a parting word concerning

Lord Mansfield, let us note that, being a Scotsman by birth, he followed, consciously or unconsciously, the Scottish tradition of cosmopolitan jurisprudence rather than the insular learning of the Inns of Court. Without that temper, made a ground of reproach against him by short-sighted enemies, the peaceful conquest of the Law Merchant by the Common Law might not have been achieved, or not so well. Certainly it was a happy day for our lady the Common Law when she took William Murray into her service; and yet we shall hardly count it mere luck. We do not refuse to ascribe merit to a sovereign who attracts the best men to his court, whether he knows or does not know precisely what their services will be. Mansfield, indeed, failed in some of his experiments which went farther on less open ground, so that two or three of his reported judgments now stand for warning rather than example. Yet nothing worse can be said of his unsuccessful ideas than that they came too late to find room in a systematic doctrine already settled.

About the same time that the annexation of the law merchant was completed, our lady began to extend her influence beyond seas in various ways. I do not speak here of the simple transport of English law by English colonists to countries where no civilized law was in possession, but only of cases where another system or tradition was there already. If, indeed, a few historical circumstances had been different, there might have been curious questions as to the local law of colonies by settlement. Nobody, for example, ever heard of a colony being under the law of Scotland, not even Nova Scotia. But what if there had been Scottish colonies before the Act of Union? At this day I conceive it may be a theoretical question what is the proper law of a ship registered in Glasgow and sailing from the Clyde. The British ensign is no more English than Scots or Irish. Under what law would a boat's crew be who landed from such a ship on an unclaimed island? The practical answer is that the modern maritime law of the two jurisdictions is identical either by statute or as part of universal sea law. But certainly there is no authority for assuming that English law, as such, is the general national maritime law of British subjects, though I have known arguments reported which seemed to make that assumption, or even to extend some such doctrine of the 'predominant partner' to the conflict of laws on land. Not that any qualified person could dispute, even in the most adventurous argument, that a conflict of this kind is just as possible between English and Scottish rules as between any others, say those of Maine and Ontario. Here, however, we are near touching on one of our lady's little secrets, or rather a family secret of all jurisprudence; namely, that any clever student can put a number of questions which lawyers and men of affairs, in the exercise of their common sense, have tacitly agreed to avoid in practice. Only one law, the Common Law, has ever gone forth into the world beyond the narrow seas under or in company with the British flag; and wherever the British flag has gone, much of the spirit of the Common Law has gone with it, if not of the letter also. Everywhere our system has made its mark, and often without official countenance. We should not expect this influence to operate alike in all parts of the law, nor to manifest itself in an invariable fashion in different and remote jurisdictions, nor do we find it so. The tendency to imitate English models is strongest in criminal and constitutional law, considerable in mercantile law; while in the private civil law of property (excluding real estate) and obligations it is less, though not negligible, and in the regions of real estate, the family and succession it hardly exists; as indeed those are not the parts of our system which any English lawyer would recommend for general adoption.   Most remarkable is the success of English criminal law, for it would be hard to name a British possession where it does not prevail under one form or another. In substance it compares not unfavourably with other systems, and this needs no proof; it is obvious that otherwise it would have no serious chance in competition.   Certainly the substantial merits of our criminal law get no help from its form.   In point of form it has almost every possible fault. It is encumbered with archaic and clumsy definitions rendered yet more obscure by centuries of judicial construction which has pursued no uniform policy.   The worst example in this kind is the definition of larceny at common law, this goes back to Bracton's adaptation (not literal copying) of Roman terms which he possibly did not understand and his successors certainly did not; and the result is that the question whether a certain act was larceny, or some other offense, or no offense at all, may be a dialectic puzzle capable of dividing judicial opinions in the last resort, involving reasons of the most subtle kind, and wholly unconnected with the merits.[1] The fruits of legislation have been little better.   Gaps have been filled up from time to time by the creation of statutory offenses, equally without any continuous plan, and often with lamentable shortcomings in both learning and draftsmanship;   and with all this accretion of legislative new matter and amendment the old misleading definitions were treated as too sacred to be touched.   Yet, strange to say, the occasions on which the difficulties come to the surface have long been so uncommon that a man may have a large

---

[1] I have known one man who thoroughly understood the law of larceny, the late Sir R. S. Wright.

criminal practice and know next to nothing of them. The Genius of the Common Law has somehow contrived to extract from all the theoretical confusion a body of law which is quite well understood by those who handle it, and quite sufficient for everyday needs, and has the reputation of being, on the whole, just and merciful.[1] Complaints almost invariably relate to the exercise of judicial discretion in sentences, especially in inferior courts, or of executive discretion in granting pardons; and I do not myself believe that any material abridgment of the judge's discretion, which certainly is very large, would in England be popular or beneficial. Thus our criminal law looks at first sight as hopeless a task for the codifier as the law of real property, but in truth lends itself to codification as well as any other branch. After that operation its intrinsic merit becomes visible, and its conquests in codified form have been extensive. Of such codes we have two types. In British India the criminal law of England was enacted in a systematic and simplified recension for a territory where the Common Law had never been in force; on the other hand, statutes have been framed for many English-speaking states with the purpose of codifying the criminal law already followed within the jurisdiction.

Now the Indian Penal Code, drawn chiefly by Macaulay more than two generations ago, has not only been in force in British India more than half a century, but has been largely copied in other countries under British rule or influence from Hong Kong to the Sudan, and among them Ceylon, where we found Roman-Dutch law in possession. In India the Company's courts had endeavoured, honestly but with no

[1] All such terms, it will be understood, are relative. We are going through something like a revolution in our notions of punishment and penal discipline, and still more of preventive measures at an early stage. These things, however, belong only in part to the domain of substantive law.

success, to adapt the penal law of the Koran, imposed by the Mogul dynasty of Delhi, to modern social conditions. It is curious to read that after Macaulay's death in 1859 Harriet Martineau, a person of universal information who was often ill-informed, pronounced his draft a complete failure. She may have taken the opinion of some philosophical Radical who disliked Whigs in general and had not forgiven Macaulay's attack on James Mill in particular. In 1860 the Penal Code was enacted, and it may be said with confidence that few codes have needed so little amendment. Turning to the other type, in which the Common Law is reduced to writing for settlers of European civilization, we find one notable parallel to the case of Ceylon. In the Province of Quebec, as we all know, the old French laws and usages of Lower Canada were preserved in civil matters, but English criminal law was introduced very soon after the British conquest, apparently without objection; and accordingly the modern Criminal Code of Canada applies to the whole of the Dominion. Mauritius gives us an example of a Crown Colony where the criminal law is English and the civil law French. In this case the circumstances were not altogether similar, as the conquest took place before the promulgation of Napoleon's codes was complete. One or two colonies have been Anglicized by degrees, beginning with criminal and public law. Trinidad is a curious, perhaps a singular, instance. This island was conquered from Spain late in the eighteenth century. The old Spanish law was administered by the first English officials, and has never been abrogated except by the piecemeal enactment, first in one branch and then in another, of rules closely following English models, or sometimes, in procedure ordinances, Anglo-Indian. By this time the whole law of the colony, civil as well as criminal, is substantially English, with one odd lacuna. Marriage, in a Spanish colony, naturally came under the exclusive jurisdiction of the Roman church. English governors could not administer Roman ecclesiastical law, nor admit the Catholic archbishop as an independent co-ordinate authority, nor yet introduce a new jurisdiction which the conscience of almost all the inhabitants would have declined to recognize. The result was that Trinidad had to do without any matrimonial jurisdiction at all. But this by the way. There seems to be no doubt that English criminal jurisprudence has an attractiveness which goes beyond the merits of its particular rules and cannot be explained by purely juridical reasons. Questions as to the rights of the citizen and the powers and duties of the magistrate may arise in almost any kind of contentious proceeding and in fact are not infrequent in civil jurisdiction. But in criminal matters they are often the only or the principal material issues; they involve graver consequences and are presented with a more dramatic emphasis. Our fathers laboured and strove chiefly in the field of Crown law to work out those ideals of public law and liberty which are embodied in the Bill of Rights and are familiar to American citizens in the constitutions of the United States and of their several commonwealths. English and American books of authority on public and particularly criminal law deal at large with these questions in many places, and the fundamental assumptions have for fully two centuries been treated as indisputable. Pleas of the Crown, to use the old English catchword, have a far higher scope than the repression of vulgar crime. Precedents of this class have varied and will continue to vary in form, as they are versed in the special institutions of British, American, Canadian or Australian government; but in every case they exhibit in action the ultimate political principles of the Common Law which belong equally to all our kindred nations. By this deeper political significance our criminal law has gained a world-wide influence in spite of its superficial technicality. Further, our criminal procedure, being associated most intimately with the elements of civic freedom as we understand them, has been not only admired, but imitated, in countries to which the Common Law is otherwise wholly foreign. The spread of trial by jury in the nineteenth century is one of the most remarkable events in the general history of legal institutions. It is not our business here to inquire whether the delicate operation of borrowing details from a foreign system has always been performed with full knowledge or with all desirable prudence.

Something remains to be said of the cases where Englishmen, or men of substantially English training and imbued with the Common Law, have been confronted with a legal system of Roman or Romanized form in the handling of ordinary civil affairs. Here the effects have been less conspicuous than in public law, but they have not been insignificant. The leading examples are those of Roman-Dutch law in South Africa (and on a smaller scale in Ceylon) and French law in the Province of Quebec. In each case the old European law which existed at the time of the British conquest has been scrupulously preserved, and whatever weight official authority has in such a matter is thrown into the same scale and against any encroachment of Common Law doctrine. Yet, in the contact of the two sets of ideas, we shall find that in each case our lady the Common Law has given rather than received. If there is a doctrine in our law more peculiar than another and less easy for a foreigner (or even a Scots lawyer) to understand, it is the doctrine of Consideration. Roughly stated, it seems plain and sensible. The Court will hold people to their bargains, but will not enforce gratuitous promises unless they are made in solemn form (and not always, or in the fullest sense of the word, then). But that was not the way in which the rules were developed, nor is the language of the authorities so simple. For ordinary business the rough statement is practically correct; the application to various unusual but not unknown cases has been made subtle and obscure by excessive dialectic refinement. Moreover the Roman law of obligations arising from contract cannot be reduced to any such general form, nor, so far as I know, the corresponding law in any modern system derived from it. Yet this particular doctrine has lately been grafted on the Roman-Dutch law in at least one South African jurisdiction. The decision does not seem elegant, and I should doubt, with great respect, whether it is useful; but the fact remains that it has been made. In the Province of Quebec things have not gone so far, but the English term has left its mark on the language, if not on the substance, of the Civil Code promulgated in our own time. This is the more notable because the lawyers and legislators of that Province are not, as a rule, men bred in the school of the Common Law. Recently a new body of law has come into being in Germany, which resembles ours in being both composite and original, but differs from it in being the product of a systematic design deliberately worked out with the best learning and skill available. There are signs that the influence of the German Civil Code in neighbouring lands, perhaps farther afield also, will make an interesting chapter of legal history before long.

Apart from the actual contents of the substantive law, it is remarkable that everywhere under the British flag—I think it

may be said without exception — our forensic and judicial
habits have prevailed. In particular the custom of attributing exclusive or all but exclusive authority to judicial
decisions, as distinguished from extra-judicial opinions of
even the most learned persons, has spread far beyond the
bounds within which English law is administered or followed. One may find indeed that imitation of our methods
is now and then carried to excess. Not only the decisions
of Indian superior courts and of the Judicial Committee on
appeal therefrom, but those of English courts, are cited
wholesale throughout British India, frequently by advocates
who cannot know much of the Common Law and before
judges or magistrates who may know as little; and the
citations, one suspects, are too often not even from the
report but at second hand from text-books. Even technical rules of English real property law have been relied on
in Indian courts without considering whether they had any
reasonable application to the facts and usage of the country.
Some Indian judges, even in the superior judgment seat
of the High Courts, have forgotten that the law they administer (with strictly limited exceptions) is not English law
as such, but 'justice, equity and good conscience,' interpreted to mean so much of English jurisprudence as appears
to be reasonably applicable, and no more. Blind following
of English precedents according to the letter can only have
the effect of reducing the estimation of the Common Law
by intelligent Indians to the level of its more technical and
less fruitful portions, and making those portions appear, if
possible, more inscrutable to Indian than they do to English
lay suitors. Still all this homage is done to the Common
Law, whether with the best of discretion or not. Neither
are the blunders our lady's fault. Like others who bear

rule in high places, she has to assume a certain measure of common sense in her officers.

It would not be wise or just to conclude, on the strength of such facts as we have rapidly surveyed, that our legal system must in itself be better or more convenient than all other actual or possible ones. But the facts, being for the more part independent of official authority or persuasion, do give proof of a certain masterful potency, not the less operative because not easy to define. Maitland found the right word for this quality. The Common Law, whatever else it may be, is pretty tough. Moralists may determine (or have determined in several irreconcilable ways) whether any and what active virtues are of a higher order or have greater merit than toughness. At all events it is of the kind that prevails.

VII. PERILS OF THE MARKET-PLACE

WE have already noticed that our law is not committed to any particular form of political institutions, but can work with any that will secure the essentials of justice and freedom. Nevertheless the form in which legal doctrine has been expressed from time to time has constantly been affected by prevailing political theories. In like manner our lady the Common Law is not a professed economist and has not (for example) any decided views about tariffs. At one time she was inclined to think that whatever a citizen's duty about domestic revenue laws might be, it was rather a laudable feat than otherwise to evade foreign ones; but this opinion is no longer of authority, if it ever was. Yet she is not without certain ideas of economic justice which her servants have endeavoured to apply 'with such consistency as they might to the circumstances of different periods. Those ideas cannot be confined within the dogmatic lines of any particular school; they cannot be invoked in favour of any universal rule of economic policy. If it be asked whether the Common Law is on the side of individual enterprise or governmental interference, we can only answer, as we did to the wider political question whether it is individualist or socialist: Both and neither. There is no doubt that the manner in which the standing principles have been worked out has been largely modified by the doctrines in favour among economists and publicists for the time being, and accordingly the tendency of decisions has inclined one

94

or another way with the fluctuations of theory. The oscil-
lations have been less violent in case-law than in legislation,
and they have followed expert opinion, or what was deemed
to be such, rather than the voice of the multitude or of a
party. For the men who make law, by judicial methods
at any rate, are not mere men in the crowd; they rather
belong to the educated class who mediate between the leaders
of thought and the general public opinion that sooner or
later follows them.

   With regard to our lady's most general principles in these
matters, they may be put very shortly. The Common
Law favours competition wherever free competition is practicable, but prefers regulation by public authority to restrictions imposed by any combination of private interests;
and this, in either case, with a view to the common advantage and not on any assumption of absolute natural rights.
Now we must be careful at the outset not to be misled into
making familiar historical words bear a purely modern significance. Free competition is favoured in the law. That
is true, but it did not originally mean unlimited competition
between all men. The merchant and the tradesman of the
Middle Ages had to be qualified persons. Before they could
exercise their business they passed through a stage of apprenticeship; and when they became 'free' of their gild or craft,
this freedom was the name (as almost always in medieval
speech) of a privileged condition, as much earned by a special
training as that of the learned professions at this day. The
man who had thus made himself a full member of a craft
or corporation had a positive right to exercise his calling or
'lawful mystery' without hindrance, and his neighbours
were entitled on their part to the benefit of his skilled work.
Our modern notion of letting every man try his chance, and

trusting unchecked competition between all sorts of competent and incompetent persons to secure the public interest automatically, may have its virtues, but it is modern and not medieval. A 'franchise' conferring an exclusive right to some kind of local profit is, of course, quite familiar in our law; one example is the exclusive right to work a ferry. Such rights might or might not be seigniorial; feudalism, that much abused antiquarian servant of all work, will not explain them. The old Common Law made no objection to the self-government of the trades, nor, with one material reservation, to the number of one trade in any one place being limited. That reservation was that the privilege must not be abused so as to create a monopoly. For the medieval fathers of the law knew well enough the danger that lay that way; they knew too that in denouncing all forms of monopoly they were supported by a strong popular feeling. It was an unlearned local court, in 1299 or 1300, that fined several chandlers of Norwich for having made a covenant among themselves that none should sell a pound of candles cheaper than another.[1] We need hardly add that presentments for breaking the assize of bread and ale and selling corrupt victual are the commonest items in both municipal and manorial records. Thus the whole system of medieval regulation hangs together. The craftsman has his rights which must be protected; it is also his duty to exercise them for the public good, and he may not disable himself from exercising them. Doubtless abundant mistakes were made in working out such a system, and some which now appear to us childish. Still it was in itself a consistent plan and by no means contemptible. It had to pass away with the condition of society for which it was made, but it left its mark in a con-

[1] Leet Jurisdiction in Norwich (Selden Soc., 1892), p. 52.

tinuing hatred of monopoly which has not lost its vigour in the latest jurisprudence and legislation of English-speaking countries; a vigour which, now as much as ever, needs to be guided by well advised judgment.

Accordingly, when monarchs in search of revenue took on themselves to grant monopolies, they found themselves in acute conflict with the people and with the lawyers; and our lady the Common Law showed, not for the first time, that she could and would maintain her ideals even against the King's authority and whatever learning he could command among his counsellors. But the danger was not exhausted here. Private and local monopolies might be created by agreement; or, short of actual monopoly, capable workers might be tempted by the offers of rivals or successors to deprive the public of their services and unduly narrow the field of competition. From these considerations the whole chapter of the law against contracts in restraint of trade was developed. In the earlier decisions, and still more in dicta which have been carelessly quoted in modern books as if they had positive authority, we find an extreme jealousy of all undertakings by which a man purports to restrain himself in any degree from the exercise of his calling. It is not clear that this attitude was always unreasonable. But as time went on the old merely local conditions disappeared, the volume and scope of trade increased, and the range of business relations in space became practically unlimited. At last it was obvious that no man dealing on a large scale could safely acquire the good-will of a business unless he were protected from destructive competition at the hands of the seller himself; without adequate protection of that kind, indeed, there really would be nothing substantial, in many kinds of business, for the seller to offer,

H

and he would find no buyers. Hence it became needful to recognize that restrictions which appeared extravagant in the sixteenth or eighteenth century might be no more than reasonable in the nineteenth; and here we may see one of our lady's most remarkable successes. Without any aid of legislation, without express disapproval of a single received authority, the law as to agreements in restraint of trade has in our own time effected a change of front that has brought it completely into line with modern business conditions. It is true that the framers of the draft Civil Code of New York inserted on this subject provisions which were much too narrow even as authority stood fifty years ago, and this with an avowed reactionary intention. Yet these clauses were adopted by the legislature of British India some ten years later, it would seem by improvidence rather than perversity. Such are the drawbacks of unconsidered imitation.

If competition under equal conditions is to be free, then it follows that the consequences must be accepted. A man cannot complain if a more skilful or fortunate competitor diminishes his profit. Monopoly is exactly what the law will not give him. It is curious that our earliest classical authority on the necessary toleration of competition relates not to rival tradesmen but to rival schoolmasters who certainly would have joined in making short work of any unqualified intruder — a process not unknown, it is said, in modern politics. This legal result fitted quite naturally, when the time came, into the political and economic theories of individual freedom which dominated the latter half of the eighteenth and the former half of the nineteenth century. Then, as the extent and variety of trafficking increase, competition assumes more complex forms, and it becomes

needful to determine the point at which competition ceases
to be fair and must be regarded as fraudulent or oppres-
sive. To enter on details here would be to undertake a
purely technical exposition both foreign to the purpose of
these lectures and useless in such a context. But it is
obvious that in a frame of society which no longer limits
competition the claim of the individual to be guaranteed
against unfair competition becomes much stronger. Indeed,
if we insisted on our institutions being or appearing logical
(as happily we do not), the individual might say with some
plausibility to the State: 'You turn us all out to compete
with one another, and say that if half of us are ruined the
other half have only exercised their common right. You
say the result is worth more to the community than it costs.
Good: but why should the cost fall wholly on innocent
unsuccessful competitors? If they suffer for the common
good, why should not the community compensate them?
Either go back to the old plan of limiting competition, or
insure us as individuals against the consequences of your
collective policy.' Thus the Nemesis of unchecked individualism would lead to something which I suppose would be
not improperly described as a form of State Socialism.
There is one answer, to be sure, which is decisive if accepted;
namely, that these matters do not concern the State at all.
It was a fashionable answer during the second and third
quarters of the nineteenth century. Whatever may be the
ultimate fate of the doctrines it sprang from (whose rise
and decline in their influence on British legislation have been
admirably set forth by my friend Professor Dicey), I do not
think this is such an answer as our lady the Common
Law has ever committed herself to, or indeed very well
could. But I must avoid the danger of putting an unli-

censed sickle into the harvest of political as distinct from legal science.

It may be worth while to notice how the doctrine of free competition has overflowed, so to speak, into the law of property. We have now held for about half a century that an occupier of land who uses it in any ordinary way is not liable, apart from claims founded on some definite special title, for any damage resulting to his neighbour. He is not bound to provide against any such result even if it is apparently probable. On the other hand, if he creates a hazardous state of things by doing anything unusual, he may fall (though not to the same extent in all jurisdictions) into the clutches of a very stringent rule [1] which recalls the most archaic law of trespass, excluding all or almost all questions of intention and negligence. This is a survival from the ancient Germanic principle that a man is liable without any qualification for the consequences ·of his voluntary acts. Where we have an original rule of this absolute kind, it is natural that the exceptions, also, when exceptions come to be recognized, should be absolute as far as they go. Thus a conception of responsibility which may be called in a relative sense primitive seems to have combined with the modern and expansive notion of individual freedom to produce a set of rules whose extremely sharp contrasts must be a cause of no little surprise to any intelligent foreign critic. On one side of a more or less conventional line I may do as I please without taking any care at all not to damage adjacent owners; on the other side I act at my peril, whatever amount of caution I may have used, or at best, according to the milder opinion held by several American courts, unless I can show that no practicable caution has been wanting.

[1] The rule in Rylands v. Fletcher.

Apart from rules of this kind, it is generally true that our law of property is individualist as between the owner and the State. The Common Law makes no provision for anything like eminent domain.[1] The king may enter on a subject's land, in time of war within the realm, for reasons of military necessity, but by way of excusable temporary intrusion, not of acquisition. He cannot compel any subject to sell him one square foot of land to improve a highway, still less grant any power of that sort to a corporation. Whatever is done in this kind nowadays (how much is done, and how helpless modern enterprise would be without it, we need not stop to mention) is done under statutory powers. The trend of all recent legislation is to magnify the office of the State in these matters. We may perhaps regret that the Common Law had no means of meeting legislation halfway: the results might have been more harmonious.

So far we have seen the law building on a foundation of common sense, medieval common sense, and yet fairly capable of adjustment to ours. But there ran along with this an assumption that wrought much mischief, and whose ghost has not ceased from troubling us, namely, that there is something intrinsically wicked in all concerted endeavour to raise the price of anything, and in particular of labour. Hence the long and lamentable history of judicial and parliamentary warfare against the persistent efforts of workmen, from the time when the medieval structure of society broke up, to devise organized methods of self-defense. A series of penal enactments from the Statute of Labourers to the latest anti-combination Acts enslaved the Common Law

[1] It has been suggested, I think by Renan, that the story of Ahab and Naboth, as we have it, is a sacerdotal libel, and Ahab was an enlightened ruler who tried to introduce 'expropriation pour cause d'utilité publiquè' to a generation too backward to understand it.

to a policy of mere repression. We were saddled with a confused and obscure doctrine of criminal conspiracy, and with a controversy not yet extinct as to the possibility of conspiracy being in itself a cause of civil action apart from any ulterior object which can be definitely called unlawful. It would be hard to find any adventure in which our lady the Common Law was worse served, or from which she came out, if she has finally come out, with less worship. Not that I think it a hopeless task to extract an acceptable opinion, so far as the common law part of the problem goes, from the seeming chaos of the books, or to show that this opinion is the better supported as well as the better in itself. On this, however, which is a matter of somewhat refined argument, I have said elsewhere what I could say. Whatever view may be taken of the technical points, there is no doubt that the law was dominated by class legislation in these matters, has paid dearly for it, and is now paying in a crude reaction. In England the last instalment of the price has been the Trade Disputes Act of 1906, a barefaced piece of retaliation which remedies some old grievances and some real or supposed new ones, not by constructing a just and comprehensive scheme on rational lines, but by creating fresh partial anomalies in the narrowest spirit of class hostility and with no regard to legal and very little to natural justice.

Another doubtful adventure of our lady the Common Law in the field of social economics has been in the theory for which our professional catchword in England is 'common employment.' Here you call it, I think more aptly, the fellow-servant doctrine. It is a very modern exception, grafted, as late as the second quarter of the nineteenth century, on the rule of an employer's liability for the acts of his servants and agents in the course of their employment.

The principal rule itself is not ancient in any general form; it was established, apparently not before the Restoration, by gradual extension from particular cases, and no record of any deliberate exposition has come down to us. When workmen and subaltern employees plucked up courage to bring actions against their masters, orthodox political economy was already in the ascendant, and those judges who had minds above mere empirical routine had one leading idea, that all would be well in the best of possible competitive worlds if one could only reduce all human relations to contract. I do not mean that they proposed to apply the same system to marriage, divorce and other domestic relations; English matrimonial jurisdiction, it will be remembered, was still in the hands of the spiritual courts. The question, therefore, which they asked without a thought of any other being admissible, was the seemingly straightforward one: What were the terms of the contract between the parties? Equity, no doubt, had pursued a different method in times past, but those, in the eyes of the philosophic reformers of 1832, were the dark uneconomic ages; and moreover it was still a pretty fixed assumption of every good common law practitioner that, when he found in equity reports anything he could not quite understand, the equity lawyer must be talking nonsense. Thus, when the workman or small clerk suffered by the negligence of a fellow-workman or a defect in the employer's plant, the judges did not search for an applicable principle of the Common Law, but relied on a short cut of infallible economic dogma. They retorted: Show us the term of your contract by which your master undertook to compensate you. This he could not do; but still he had a reply. Show me, he said in effect, the term by which I have undertaken to waive the common

right of holding a master to answer for his servant's negligence. But the Court, having gone so far, did not stick
at the further step of implying as against the workman a
term which was not there. That risk, they said, must have
been counted in fixing your wages. It was not a convincing
reply to the workman: it hardly seems convincing to the
majority of thoughtful lawyers at this day. Such as it was,
it dominated English jurisprudence for a generation, and is
still of authority so far as not displaced by statute. Now
I am not speaking here of England alone. In fact, our first
leading case did not raise the question squarely. It was a
Massachusetts case in which, within a few years, Chief
Justice Shaw fairly took it in hand, and laid down the
'fellow-servant doctrine' in one of his most able judgments.
I do not think the later authorities (including the decisions
by which the House of Lords forced the doctrine on Scotland in its full extent) go much beyond repeating his reasons
with variations. This doctrine, I humbly conceive, has been
one of the great mistakes of the Common Law. Starting
to handle the problem on the ground of contract and of contract alone, our Victorian lawyers found no real agreement
at all on the point in dispute, and stultified their own initial
assumption by inventing one. It is a sad example of the
wrong way to use fiction. And yet this was the same generation of judges who introduced the brilliant, eminently just
and wholly successful fiction that a professed agent warrants
his authority. Being once established, the perverse doctrine
was worked out with relentless logical ability, for the most
part in the Court of Exchequer, a court which in our fathers'
time had great qualities and the defects of those qualities.
Even of late years the results have been seen in a few cases
of this class where for some inscrutable reason plaintiffs

have chosen to risk an action at common law. No plain man would say that an actor's employment has much in common with a scene-shifter's. It is not an actor's business to understand the stage machinery; he has no right to interfere in handling it, and would be neglecting his own duties if he attempted to observe how the work was being done. Nevertheless it is held that if a scene-shifter in the flies drops a heavy object on the actor's head, they are fellow-servants of the manager in a common employment, and the actor cannot recover.

A rule so manifestly one-sided and so remote from ordinary notions of justice could not stand unamended. It is hardly worth while at this day to consider whether some less extensive doctrine on similar lines might have been tolerable. For example, it might have been held that the employer (having used due diligence in finding competent workmen) should not be liable to one workman for the negligence of others employed along with him in the same operation and in a grade not above his own. What was in fact held was that the rule of liability for servants' negligence exists only for the protection of the outside public, and has nothing to do with what goes on inside the employer's undertaking, however various its branches and how many soever the degrees of authority and responsibility may be. The case-law of several American states has, I believe, more or less qualified the doctrine in the direction above suggested; I do not know whether such modifications have anywhere been accepted as adequate. On the whole the Common Law had come to a deadlock, and about thirty years ago the period of remedial legislation set in. As usual, the first experiment was empirical and clumsy. Nothing could be much worse in point of form than our Employers' Liability Act of 1880, which mitigated an anomalous rule by creating

an involved series of exceptions and sub-exceptions, further
complicated by minute novelties in procedure. However,
it was better than nothing, and has, I believe, been rather
widely imitated. All this does not touch the real economic
problem. From the business point of view it is not a question of individual wrongs, but of insurance on a large scale.
If the fellow-servant doctrine had never been invented,
employers would have accepted the risk and, when it became considerable, insured against it. The mere lawyer
must be excused from determining in what proportions the
insurance would ultimately rest on the employer, or fall on
the workman in the shape of diminished wages, or on the
consumer of the product (anything from an Atlantic liner
to an opera) in the shape of enhanced prices. Even so,
however, there would remain the difficulty that there is no
cause of legal action without proof of negligence somewhere,
and that such proof is often troublesome and precarious.
In 1897 our Parliament, inspired by Joseph Chamberlain,
took the bold course of removing the whole matter out of
the litigious region where the first necessary step is to find
some person in default. Our Workmen's Compensation
Act makes the employer an insurer not against negligence
as such, but against accidents, and leaves him to insure over.
This, to go back for a moment upon a question already put,
may for anything I know be socialism. Certainly some
people take pleasure in calling it so: which, in my poor
judgment, makes it neither better nor worse. With or without this or any other classifying label, it deserves the credit
of being a courageous endeavour to get behind the technical
categories and attack the problem in its real center. In
point of form the Act is not a satisfactory piece of work.
The use of semi-popular language resembling terms already

known to the law but not identical with them has led, as it always does, to tedious and inconclusive controversies on points of construction, in which the real dispute is nine times out of ten on the minute interpretation of the facts. One may hope that this fault, and others which I cannot stop to explain here, may be avoided in other jurisdictions.

We have seen by these examples that the Common Law has passed or is passing through at least three distinct stages of economic assumption in its dealings with industrial affairs and the relations of capital and labour. There was the medieval stage in which every man was supposed to have his proper state of life, and the law had to see that he.was kept in it. We cannot fix a point of time when this conception of social welfare ceased to be officially accepted. Official and judicial opinion are rather apt to lag behind the general movement of ideas, but they do move, and older and younger colleagues are not likely to move at the same pace : just as, in dating a manuscript, one has to remember that an ancient scribe may be writing the hand of the last generation at the same time that a young one is eager to display the very newest graces of penmanship. We shall not be far wrong in placing the period of transition between the beginning of the nineteenth century and the reforms of 1832. Next came the reign of utilitarian individualism, under which unlimited competition was to be the universal regulator, and it was thought that the State ought not to hinder [this beneficent operation of human nature and could do nothing to help it beyond removing artificial obstacles. In the faith of that doctrine our fathers (I mean the fathers of men now growing old) lived through their active years, and their sons were brought up in its atmosphere. It prevailed for approximately half a century. Then, well within the memory of men not much past the prime of life, it became a tolerated, indeed a probable or plausible, opinion, that the State was abdicating its functions by remaining passive, and should not only leave the road open for ability, but give active assistance in suppressing unfavourable external conditions and equalizing opportunities. The present generation is full of this spirit, and its power seems likely to increase for some time yet. It is not for me to discuss the merits of these different ideals or to point out the perversions and excesses incident to each of them. What we have to note is that in a community pervaded by any of them the law runs no small danger of accepting the current opinion without any critical examination and importing it into judgments that ought to be purely legal. I do not know why lawyers should be readier than other men to take persons holding themselves out as experts at their own valuation, but so it is that they are generally credulous in matters outside their own art, except when they are cross-examining a hostile expert witness; and our lady the Common Law pays for it sooner or later. The conclusion is that judges ought to be very careful about committing themselves to fashionable economic theories: first because they are quite likely to misunderstand or misapply such theories, secondly because the theory may well be discredited after a short time, and thirdly because, when mistakes in this kind are once made, they are pretty sure to call for legislation, and the legislative amendment is almost sure to be unsatisfactory.

We have been speaking of particular failures in the face of social and industrial conflicts, doing our best neither to exaggerate nor to extenuate. It would be disloyal to our lady if we left off on this note without saying a word of her success in keeping her more general methods up to the mark of business requirements. We are so familiar with our learning of Agency, now a common learning in all essentials, that we seldom stop to think how much we owe to its rapid, comprehensive, and elastic development in the course of the past century. Beginning with very simple principles, it has grown to be capable of dealing with the most intricate commercial relations and finding solutions acceptable to men of business as just, and to lawyers as workmanlike and scientific. It has enabled us to build up a full and elaborate law of corporations and reserve the thorny speculative problem of corporate personality to be discussed in such learned leisure as we may command, without any fear of unsettling practical foundations. Combined with the equitable doctrine of notice, it has allowed us to enforce the highest standard of honesty and diligence in dealings with every kind of property. If the law has sometimes erred in refinement, it is a fault on the better side. Another weapon of great power is in our lady's hand for maintaining good faith in all kinds of business, the doctrine of Estoppel, a subtle and far-reaching weapon not to be wielded without skill and judgment, but such is the virtue of all arms of precision. We may safely challenge any other system to show principles of like generality better fitted to advance justice, capable of nicer discrimination in doubtful affairs, or applied with more scientific elegance. A man who has mastered these two branches of our jurisprudence, Agency and Estoppel, may not always, in a complex piece of business, give that opinion which finally prevails in court, but he will surely give one that has to be treated with respect. Equipped with such arms, our lady the Common Law may take to herself the praise of the lover in the Song of Songs. Her justice is fair as the moon, clear as the sun and terrible as an army with banners.

VIII. THE PERPETUAL QUEST

In the foregoing lectures we have surveyed a certain number of our lady the Common Law's adventures, prosperous and otherwise. The stories I have tried to recall to memory rather than to tell anew are only a selection. It is quite likely that other men whose attention has been more particularly given to other branches of the law and its history might make other selections not less interesting and profitable. Accordingly, whatever the result may properly be called, it can hardly claim to make any systematic addition to the knowledge of our legal antiquities, and the legal antiquary who looks for anything of that kind will be disappointed, and may perhaps even accuse us of frivolity. We shall bear any such charge with equanimity, for the short reason that we did not go about to satisfy that kind of curiosity at all. The Common Law is not a museum of antiquities, but a living and active law, and our purpose has been to exhibit in the light of their past effects the faculties, the operations and the perils which to-day as much as ever enter into that life. I have no objection to antiquarian zeal; I own to a share of it myself. Antiquaries are for the most part good harmless folks enough, and when they excommunicate one another, about cuneiform records or the origins of Ægean civilization, it is only their domestic amusement. But we did not go out to collect fossils this time. I do not want you to remember anything of what we have seen together save so far as it bears on

110

the attitude of modern lawyers towards the perfectly living problems of their science and calling. There is only one opinion against which I have to take a stand of positive contradiction, the opinion, if any one seriously maintains it, that there is some date at which you can draw a line and say: Here modern law begins, and only professors of legal history need know anything that lies behind it. There is no such line. You need not have read the Anglo-Saxon dooms or possess Dr. Liebermann's edition of them, but if you have heard nothing of either you may some day be quite practically baffled by an adversary talking non-sense about Anglo-Saxon institutions which you cannot see through and answer. You need not make a minute study of medieval French, but one day your client's interest may well depend on your ability to expose an inaccurate translation from a Year Book. But these, some one will say, are the extraordinary chances of the profession. If such things do come, why should they come to me? and is it worth my while to be ready for them? Perhaps not, we should answer, if you have made up your mind to expect nothing from your profession but food and shelter not falling below a certain standard of decency, and rising, if fortune will, to a fair share of the world's luxuries: as to which the measure and vicissitudes of the various degrees, from clambake to champagne, from a catboat round Cape Cod to a yacht round the Mediterranean, will interest nobody but yourself. But if you have any ambition, then it is most certainly worth your while. In every calling, without exception that I know of, the difference between the merely adequate journeyman and the accomplished craftsman who is really master of his art is that the journeyman knows what to do with the usual task, but the artist knows what to do with an unusual one. The true craftsman may wait long for his opportunity, but when it comes he will never be taken for a journeyman again. It is the difference between being a slave of current rules, helpless outside their range, and using them as tools with mastery of the principles on which they depend; the same difference that shows itself on the highest planes of conduct and insight between ordinary good men and heroes or saints. Or, to put it in the most modest terms, the difference is between performance of the part that falls to you such that, as they say in New England, you guess it will have to do, and a performance that counts. And on the whole really good work does count even in this world.

Let it be granted then that we speak as among lawyers who have some professional ambition. I do not care whether its aim stops at acquiring the reputation of being a good lawyer, and being one as the surest way thereto, with the consequent prospect of advancement, or is touched, as I hope it often is, with the desire of justifying one's profession before the world's judgment and leaving the science of the law in some way better than one found it. What shall be the attitude of a good lawyer and a good citizen towards the problems among which the lot of the Common Law is cast? He will recognize, in the first place, that they are alive and not to be solved out of a digest, and that the work is never finished. If it ever seemed to be finished, the law would have ceased to be a living science and would be fit for nothing more than to be petrified in an official Corpus Juris. For principles, even the most certain, are capable of infinite application, and the matter is always changing. The knights errant of our lady the Common Law must be abroad on a perpetual quest; no sooner is an adventure accomplished than a fresh one is disclosed or arises out of that very achievement. There is no strife in the past which has not some lesson for the future. Look back to the first point of our survey; does any one suppose that the great fight with formalism is over? There may be some happy jurisdiction (I do not know where it may be found) in which pleading is effectually reformed and statutes are few and simple. Let it be so, but one or two jurisdictions do not account for the Common Law. Formalism may be driven out of pleading, there may be no arguable points left on rules of procedure, but the hydra heads have their own devilish immortality, and will be grinning at you again in captious perversions of statute law. Courts have to be guided, legislators have to be warned. Not a word shall be said here in derogation of an advocate's duty to take every point that can fairly be taken for his client. Still there is a higher and a lower kind of advocacy, including work out of court, without any prejudice to the client's interest. Not long ago a learned friend of Lincoln's Inn was talking with me of a late eminent English conveyancing counsel whose pupil he had been, and whom he had often met later in conference. Other men might be as learned, said my friend, but I worked much with him, and whoever worked with him might be sure that he wanted to put the business through. That is in plain words, which no rhetorical expansion could better, the spirit of the law and the true lawyer. Ask yourself at every doubtful turn: What will best help the business through? and you will have a good professional conscience and grateful clients.

Again there is a danger much akin to formalism and always besetting us. Our system is founded on precedent and respect for authorities. But this just and necessary respect,

I

if not informed by a due measure of intelligent criticism, tends to degenerate into mechanical slavery. Perhaps that kind of corruption is harder to avoid in a country of uniform and centralized jurisdiction like England than under a federal constitution where judiciary power is distributed among many co-ordinate and independent courts, but the temptation exists everywhere. I have already mentioned its influence in British India. Practitioners bred to the Common Law and speaking its language as their mother tongue have less excuse than Indian pleaders. If they have learnt their trade rightly, they should have learnt to weigh as well as to count authorities. Any man who knows how to handle the professional apparatus of reference can find, with moderate industry, something like a show of authority for almost anything : and it is the delight of a certain class of advocates to snatch an advantage (though it is apt to be a fleeting one) by this method. But the law is not made by casual and hasty decisions in courts of first instance. Its guiding principles and the harmony of its controlling ideas must be sought in the considered judgments of the higher tribunals which command universal respect ; and whatever is contrary to the general consent of leading authorities ought to be frankly discarded as erroneous. In any particular jurisdiction, to be sure, one may be bound by a particular eccentric doctrine which has gained an undeserved reception : such unfortunate accidents must be endured. Herein we may have also to face a temptation of the higher kind, such as theologians hold to be among the trials of the elect. A learned judge or text-writer often finds it a fascinating intellectual exercise to reconcile all the authorities bearing or seeming to bear on a given point ; and with this purpose (which in itself is laudable enough) solutions of extreme ingenuity and subtilty are advanced. You may find striking examples in the work of a very learned English author whom the profession has recently lost, Mr. Thomas Beven. There comes a point however where such exercises of erudition serve only to 'make that darker which was dark enough without.' I venture to offer a rough working test. When you find an elaborate harmony of all the decisions expressed in a formula which it would be impossible to explain to a jury, then you may suspect that some of the decisions are wrong; and it may be the more profitable course in every sense to consider, not how you can fit them all into a Chinese puzzle of rules, sub-rules, exceptions, and sub-exceptions, but which of them are least likely to hold their own before a court of last resort. If you can find a conclusion which appears to be the most conformable to principles and rules already settled; if that conclusion does not seem to lead to any such inconvenience as calls for exceptional treatment; and if, on the balance of judicial opinion, it is supported by the weight of binding or persuasive authorities in your own and other leading jurisdictions, then you had better make up your mind that refined qualifications will not easily be fastened on it. Certainly these questions may well be *inter apices juris* and divide the most learned opinions. Yet there must be a more and a less promising way of approaching them, and I think the sounder attitude of mind is that which I have indicated. Sometimes it may be necessary to frame an argument against the application of that which one suspects to be the better opinion in law (I say suspects because, as Dr. Johnson rightly observed, you have no business to think you know it until the Court has decided). In such a case the prudent advocate will, if he can, throw his strength in the direction of arguing on the facts that the rule does not apply rather than commit himself to a battle of pure law in an unfavourable position.   There is yet another temptation of the elect, and I think it is the most insidious of all, judged by the number of cases in which competent and even eminent persons have yielded to it.   I mean the habit of admitting exceptions and anomalies in detail on the ground of immediate convenience.   Oftentimes the sum of many such little concessions to convenience is the grave inconvenience of nobody knowing whether any rule at all is left.   I do not deny that, if the original rule was a bad one, this way of escape from it may be better than none.   But in a question of this kind it may very well turn out, on careful examination, that the principal rule has been too narrowly conceived or expressed, and that when it is rightly apprehended, no exception has to be made in order to arrive at a reasonable result.   It is always worth while to give one's best consideration to the authorities from this point of view.

Another object for which we can all do something, for there are so many ways of helping that any man may find at least one pretty near his hand, is that of keeping the movement of our native jurisprudence to its proper lines.   Our lady the Common Law will note other people's fashions and take a hint from them in season, but she will have no thanks for judges or legislators who steal incongruous tags and patches and offer to bedizen her raiment with them.   Assimilation of foreign elements, we have already seen, may be a very good thing.   Crude and hasty borrowing of foreign details is unbecoming at best, and almost always mischievous. When you are tempted to make play with foreign ideas or terms, either for imitation or for criticism, the first thing is to be sure that you understand them.   Nothing is easier than to misunderstand little bits of another system.   One may read in very learned English authors that there is no specific performance in French law, for which these authors proceed to give every reason except the real one. The matter is really quite simple. Modern French law has done for the sale of all kinds of property what the Common Law did in the Middle Ages for the sale of ascertained goods, made a complete contract of sale pass the whole legal interest without any further act of transfer. Thus the purchaser is at once owner; and, being armed with all the rights and remedies of an owner, he has no need of any such remedy as our action for specific performance of a contract to sell real estate. Those learned persons, again, having overlooked the general provisions of the French law as to sale, naturally failed to see its incidents in the proper light, and put questions to learned Frenchmen which they in turn, knowing nothing of our peculiar law of property nor the mysteries of the legal estate, did not rightly apprehend. Hence one may draw the moral of a supplemental warning. Beware of putting categorical questions to a foreign expert without explaining to him the general bearing of your inquiry and the conditions taken for granted by English-speaking lawyers. Otherwise you may get an answer that is literally correct but substantially misleading, and discover too late that you have been talking at cross purposes. Then comes the case where you think to find some profit in imitation. Here the next thing, after you have mastered the foreign matter, is to have a clear view of the end to be served by taking it as a model, and to make sure whether it cannot be served as well or better by methods already known to our own law.

A fair specimen of what ought to be avoided may be found in the English Act commonly called Lord Campbell's Act, and now officially cited by the not wholly accurate

short title of the Fatal Accidents Act. The example is convenient because this Act has been widely imitated in other
jurisdictions, and none the worse because it has been useful
in spite of its defects, and is not involved with any burning
social or economic question. In its infancy the Common Law
knew nothing of executors and very little of wills. The
testament of personal estate, and therefore the executor,
were introduced by ecclesiastical jurisdiction, although the
executor has a fine old Germanic pedigree. So the right of
an executor to sue in the king's courts for the benefit of his
testator's estate was brought in piecemeal and not without
help of statutes. Most unluckily some one got hold of a
supposed Roman maxim, for which there is really no authority, that 'personal actions die with the person.' By
further ill luck an opinion for which classical Roman warrant
does exist came to reinforce this pretended authority, the
opinion that a free man's life is incapable of pecuniary valuation. It is a fine ethical observation, but, I venture to think,
inappropriate in the field of legal justice. In the result, the
Common Law was saddled with the rule that the death of a
human being cannot give rise to a civil cause of action, one
of the most foolish rules, if I dare say so, that have ever
been adopted by the courts of a civilized country; and we
have to learn for law that, except for statutory exceptions,
and apart from criminal liability, a man wounds or disables
another at his peril,[1] but may kill him outright with im-
punity. Surely a wise legislature might have made a clean
piece of work and repealed the apocryphal maxims altogether.
Instead of this our Parliament was advised to borrow from

[1] Subject, in modern law, to divers causes of justification and excuse which
ancient law did not recognize; but these distinctions are not relevant to the
matter now in hand.

Scotland provisions which, for aught I know, may have a perfectly fit place in the body of Scottish law, and to confer an anomalous cause of action, not on the legal representative of the deceased person who might have brought an action himself if he had not been killed, but directly on a class of persons who might be presumed to suffer by his death as being dependent on him. In other cases the absurdity of the general rule remained uncorrected; our Court of Appeal has held it too inveterate to be touched; and there is no prospect of rational and comprehensive legislation.

We may take another example from the theoretical study of the Common Law. During the nineteenth century it was rather fashionable for speculative writers to assume that the Roman doctrine of Possession was more complete and scientific than our own. This, I believe, was only because they had not taken the pains to grapple with the authorities of our law on trespass, disseisin, trover and possessory remedies generally. It may be admitted that the labour would have been considerable; certainly I found it so when I tried my own hand, even with the most valuable help which I derived from working in association with my learned friend the late Mr. Justice Wright, who had made a special study of the subject with reference to the criminal law. The result, however, was to show that the doctrine of Possession in the Common Law, scattered as it is in various decisions partly in civil and partly in criminal jurisdiction, and arising out of the most varied facts and transactions, can be accounted for by a few comprehensive principles which are both more elegant and in closer touch with the conditions of actual life than any of the formulas which the ingenuity of modern commentators has extracted from the sayings of the classical Roman jurists. In these lectures I have purposely avoided

any technical exposition, yet for the honour of our lady the
Common Law I will state these principles in their simplest
form. First, possession in fact is such actual exclusive
control as the nature of the thing, whatever it may be, admits. Secondly, possession in law, the right which is protected by possessory remedies, generally follows possession
in fact, but does not necessarily cease when possession in
fact ceases. The chief exception to this rule is that a
servant in charge of his master's goods has not possession in
law; and reflection shows that, whatever the origin of this
exception may be, it conforms to common sense; for in fact
a servant not only is bound to exercise his physical control
according to his master's will, as and when it is signified,
and not his own, but in ordinary cases he does not even appear to be dealing with the thing in his own right, and no
man using common attention and judgment would suppose
that he claimed any such right. Thirdly, possession in law
continues until determined in some way which the law definitely recognizes, beyond the mere absence or failure of a
continuing intent to possess. Fourthly, possession in law is a
commencement of title, in other words the possessor can deal
with the thing as an owner against all persons not having a
better title, and this protection extends to persons deriving
title from him in good faith. Fifthly, when possession in fact
is so contested that no one can be said to have actual effective
control, possession in law follows the better title. It is true
that every one of these principles, in its application to the
complex facts of life, may call for careful and even subtle
elaboration. But I am free to maintain that in themselves
they are adequate and rational. We take the line of making
legal possession coincide with apparent control so far as
possible; the Roman law takes the opposite line of unwilling-

ness to separate legal possession from ownership or what we call 'general property'; and I venture to think our way both the simpler and the better. It is fortunate that our courts were never beguiled by Continental learning, well or ill understood, into departure from our native line of advance; and it does not matter how much of their refusal to listen to any voice of Roman charmers was due to deliberate wisdom, and how much to pure ignorance of the voluminous and controversial literature which, so far as I know, has not yet produced any generally accepted theory in modern Roman law. Not that the Roman law is to be neglected by those who have time to attend to it, for it furnishes many instructive parallels, still more instructive contrasts, and many ingenious suggestions. But there is no reason for believing that our Germanic ideas of seisin, from which our native doctrine has sprung, have in them less of the true root of the matter.

At this point, or earlier, I am sure a reflection will have occurred to you which at first sight is discouraging. All we have heard, you will say, may be very true. We are willing to believe that the general course of a lawyer who wishes to do credit to his art has been indicated on sound lines. But when we come to face an actual problem in its complexity, will any such monitions make us sure of handling it in the right way? Now it would be neither wise nor honest to shirk this question. The answer is quite plain : They will not. The same answer holds in all science and art whatsoever. No one else can do your own work for you, and no one can learn to do anything worth doing by so cheap a way as hearing or reading about it. Apprenticeship is the only road to craftsmanship, and no man can expect to learn without making mistakes. But the experience of elders

may at least help you to start in the right direction and
to avoid perverse and gratuitous errors. Reading the map
will never get a man up a mountain, but the prudent climber
will not therefore omit to study the best map available.
Our maps are not perfect, but they are good enough to be
useful.

And now that we have followed our lady the Common
Law through vicissitudes of success and failure, walking
with her familiarly, not slavishly, how does it stand with
our affection for her? Shall we be tempted to belittle her
work because it is in rough and stubborn material, and
all the toil of her servants has not wholly purified
the fine gold from the dross? There was a great English writer, one who had gone through the forms of study-
ing the law and was nominally qualified to practise. He
wrote an excellent description of life in the Temple as
it was in his youth; his name was Thackeray. He drew
the picture of a student wholly absorbed in his profession,
in contrast to the diversions of Pendennis and his friend
Warrington, and this is what he said of Mr Paley, the type
of an industrious and concentrated lawyer, a type we have
all seen more or less realized in the flesh: 'How differently
employed Mr. Paley has been! He has not been throwing
himself away: he has only been bringing a great intellect
laboriously down to the comprehension of a mean subject.'[1] I venture to pronounce these words not worthy
of Thackeray. Mr. Paley's way of handling the subject
might be mean; that gives no man a right to call the subject itself mean. Even so, I am apt to think Mr. Paley may
be maligned. Every man who takes his profession seriously
must be content for a time to give his whole mind to it and

[1] Pendennis, ch. xxix.

think of little else, not to abolish his other interests (which would be the worse for his profession in the end), but to restrain or suspend them for a while. How did Pendennis and Warrington know what other and unselfish objects Mr. Paley might be working for? How could they be certain that he had not a mother or sisters looking to him for support? Did they see anything of his pursuits and. recreations in vacation time? One very learned person of Lincoln's Inn, who might in a superficial way have sat for Mr. Paley's portrait, was known in the Alpine Club about fifty years ago as a member of the party which made one of the most daring expeditions in the Bernese Oberland in the Club's heroic age of conquest. His one besetting fault was an excess of conscientiousness from which no one suffered so much as himself. But let Thackeray's lapse pass, a mere slip of the pen I would fain think, for in truth he was a man of a generous nature and would not have written so in malice. Macaulay's lament over Fearne's devotion of a lifetime to 'the barbarous puzzle of contingent remainders' was better justified. As to that I will merely say that our lady the Common Law is not answerable for the Statute of Uses and all the puzzles and perplexities it brought in its train. We shall not think the less of her for not being infallible and invincible. Some say she is a hard mistress. It is true that she will not be content with any offering short of a man's best work: she would not be faithful to herself if she were. Some call her capricious. It is true that she does not undertake to command worldly success for her followers; earthly fortune may be added to them, but is not the reward she promises. There are some who call her arbitrary. True it is that we have to learn her speech, but when we have learnt enough of it to speak it freely we know that open discussion and unfettered criticism are the very life of the law. Some complain of her tongue as barbarous. Well, the Latin of Roman law falls short, at best, of classical perfection, and when one gets below the surface of our medieval books, French and Latin, one finds them at least as human as the Digest and far more living and human than Justinian's Institutes and the glossators. Rather we may praise our lady the Common Law in the words of a poet who was not a lawyer, words not written concerning her, and nevertheless appropriate.

> Our lady of love by you is unbeholden;
> For hands she hath none, nor eyes, nor lips, nor golden
>   Treasure of hair, nor face nor form ; but we
>   That love, we know her more fair than anything.

Now this was written by Algernon Charles Swinburne in praise of Liberty at a time when the powers of darkness were still very strong on the Continent of Europe. There is ample warrant in medieval usage for appropriating verses of any author in one's own sense, whether connected with that author's or not; and our lady's traditions are nothing if not medieval. But we may find a less artificial justification. For if there is any virtue in the Common Law whereby she stands for more than intellectual excellence in a special kind of learning, it is that Freedom is her sister, and in the spirit of freedom her greatest work has ever been done. By that spirit our lady has emboldened her servants to speak the truth before kings, to restrain the tyranny of usurping license, and to carry her ideal of equal public justice and ordered right into every quarter of the world. By the fire of that spirit our worship of her is touched and enlightened, and in its power, knowing that the service we render to her is freedom, we claim no inferior fellowship with our brethren of the other great Faculties, the healers of the body and the comforters of the soul, the lovers of all that is highest in this world and beyond.   There is no more arduous enterprise for lawful men, and none more noble, than the perpetual quest of justice laid upon all of us who are pledged to serve our lady the Common Law.

INDEX

K

Rents reserved on conveyances in fee simple in Pennsylvania, 50

Replication *de injuria* in full force in New Jersey, 29

Rescue and ransom, 59–74

"Respondeat superior," Example of, in sheriff's responsibility, 46

Restraint of trade, Development of law against, 96, 97, 98

Revolutions and the civil law, 55

Rhadamanthus, Court of, in "Crogate's Case," 29

Riot abnormal, 38

Ritual, Forms of, need not be invariable, 15–16; æsthetic history of, left to anthropologists, 16; judicial results of a semi-magical, ceased to be tolerable, 21

Rogers, Showell, "The Ethics of Advocacy," 46n

Roman law of obligation arising from contract, 91

Roman-Dutch law in Ceylon, 87; and in South Africa, 90–91; Doctrine of consideration grafted on the, 91

Romanist importation in jurisprudence, 80

Royal justice, Conflict of, with lawlessness, 39–41

Rylands *v.* Fletcher, The rule in, 100

St. German, "Doctor and Student," 81

St. Mary-le-Bow in the ward of Cheap, 71

Saxons, The, of Britain, 12

Scandinavians among our heathen ancestors, 10

Schoolmasters, Competition and, 98

Schoolmen, The accepted teaching of the, 11

Scotland, Law of, and English law, 84–85

Scottish rules, Conflict between English and, possible, 85

Seisin, Germanic ideas of, 121

Selden, John, Unique learning and judgment of, 76

Shakespeare, License taken by, in suit of Shylock, 18

Shaw, Chief Justice, Judgment of,

in fellow-servant doctrine case, 104

Sheriff, A good, in Middle Ages, 40; responsibility of, to people, 46

Smith, Sir Thomas, on insolency of North of England noblemen, 41

Social legislation promoted for party interests, 48–49

Social welfare, Medieval conception of, 107

Socialism calls for more legal compulsion, 51; confused with anarchism, 55; constitution of the family a matter appertaining to, 54; discouragement of private law under, 51; a strike under, would be a rebellion 52; and free competition, 99

Socialism, State, Unchecked individualism would lead to a form of, 99

Socialists demand more legal compulsion, 51–52; some, really anarchists, 52–53

Specific performance, Why no action for, in modern French law, 117

Star Chamber, The King's Council in the, 41; jurisdiction of, 45; criminal jurisdiction in, 66; made an engine of persecution by Charles I, 66

State, The, and competition, 99; should equalize opportunities, 108

State legislation, Encroachments of, on legal jurisdiction, 43

State secrets must be protected by jurisprudence, 12

Statute of Frauds, 83

Statute of Labourers, 48, 101

Statute of Uses, 50–51; common law not answerable to, 123

Statute of Wards and Liveries, 50

Statute of Westminster, The, 44

Statutes, modern, Tendency of, to encroach on legal jurisdiction, 43

Stephen on Pleading, 26n1

Stonore, Judge, on law, 2

Strike, A, in a socialist State, a rebellion, 52

Stuarts, Loss of power by the, 13

Substantial justice, 32n1

Subtilty for subtilty's sake, 26; the vice of, 35

C. ALEX NELSON